THE SECRET LIVES OF
GARDEN BEES

This book is dedicated to my wonderful mum, Betty, who shared her love of nature and the beauty of small things.

Dearly missed, but never forgotten.

THE SECRET LIVES OF
GARDEN BEES

JEAN VERNON

WHITE OWL
AN IMPRINT OF PEN & SWORD BOOKS LTD.
YORKSHIRE – PHILADELPHIA

First published in Great Britain in 2020 and reprinted in 2020 by
Pen and Sword WHITE OWL
An imprint of
Pen & Sword Books Ltd
Yorkshire - Philadelphia

Hardback ISBN: 978 1 52671 186 1
Paperback ISBN: 978 1 52676 651 9

A CIP catalogue record for this book is available from the British Library.

Typeset in 11/14 pts Cormorant Infant
by Aura Technology and Software Services, India.

Printed and bound in India by Replika Press Pvt. Ltd.

Pen & Sword Books Ltd incorporates the Imprints of Pen & Sword Books Archaeology, Atlas, Aviation, Battleground, Discovery, Family History, History, Maritime, Military, Naval, Politics, Railways, Select, Transport, True Crime, Fiction, Frontline Books, Leo Cooper, Praetorian Press, Seaforth Publishing, Wharncliffe and White Owl.

For a complete list of Pen & Sword titles please contact

PEN & SWORD BOOKS LIMITED
47 Church Street, Barnsley, South Yorkshire, S70 2AS, England
E-mail: enquiries@pen-and-sword.co.uk
Website: www.pen-and-sword.co.uk

or

PEN AND SWORD BOOKS
1950 Lawrence Rd, Havertown, PA 19083, USA
E-mail: Uspen-and-sword@casematepublishers.com
Website: www.penandswordbooks.com

Contents

Foreword

Considering the enormous debt we humans owe bees, it is surprising how little most of us actually know about them. Ask the average person on the street what springs to mind when you mention the word 'bee', and most will reply "honey", "swarms" or "stings". Dig a little deeper and some might acknowledge the important roles they play as pollinators, or talk affectionately about the fuzzy bumblebees that visit their gardens, but only rarely will anyone mention 'solitary bees' or, in fact, even be aware of their existence.

It is only in the last ten years or so that I have become aware of the vast numbers and diversity of bee species we share this planet with. With each passing year I have become more fascinated by these enchanting little insects – their lifecycles, their behaviour and skills, the ways in which social species interact with each other, and the complex relationships they have with flowering plants. They are, quite simply, extraordinary. As well as all this, bees have opened a window for me into the wider world of nature. Because of them I now pay greater attention to the flowers they forage upon and all the other insects that feed alongside them. They are my harbingers of spring, and the sounds of my summer. For all the months of the year that bees are on the wing, I watch them, follow them, photograph them, read about them... and never tire of learning more about their ways. I miss them sorely over winter.

Jean Vernon understands all of this. She, too, has fallen more than a little in love with these wondrous creatures. If I didn't know this already of Jean, I would know it from the way she writes in this beautiful book – in particular from the way she describes the bees, and other insects, she has come across in her own garden and farther afield.

Written from the heart, but with great care and attention to detail, *The Secret Lives of Garden Bees* is packed with fascinating information and delightful insights into the hidden world of garden bees. It contains practical advice on how we can all do our bit to welcome and encourage bees to visit our own gardens, as well as other nuggets and tips about how to help bees, which extend way beyond the usual lists of 'what to plant'. And all of this presented in such an accessible, gently humorous and 'gardener-friendly' way. Oh how I wish this book had been around when I first became interested in bees!

It has been most encouraging, over the last few years, to witness people's concern and determination to help our beleaguered pollinators. This has resulted in a growing interest in 'gardening for bees' and, more recently, a shift towards people becoming more aware of the bees themselves. In fact, as I write, twitter and instagram are positively buzzing with photographs of 'Leaf-cutter' bees carrying carefully cut pieces of rolled up leaves, or flower petals, back to their nests, and conversations about how and where these charming little bees are building their nests. The thirst for knowledge is almost palpable. Jean's book could not be more timely.

The thing that makes this book stand out from other books about bees, apart from the fact that it is not all about honeybees, is the way in which Jean weaves together her unabashed love of bees, with her understanding of their individual and collective needs. In it, she invites us to 'meet the bees', singling out some of the more easily identifiable species that we are likely to find in our gardens – such as the strikingly handsome Red-tailed bumblebee, the smaller, but equally stunning Tawny and Ashy Mining bees, and (you will be pleased to know) the much talked about Leaf-cutter bees. She also introduces us to less common species, including the Bilberry bumblebee and the Long-horned bee, both famed for their beauty, but also both, sadly, declining in range and numbers.

Jean's wonderful descriptions of these, and other bees, together with the glorious colour photographs throughout, bring the bees in this book to life. It has been a pleasure and a joy to read, and I hope you enjoy it as much as I have.

Brigit Strawbridge Howard
Shaftesbury, Dorset.

2nd August 2019

Starting with bees

I'm not quite sure when I first fell in love with bees, or even when I first noticed them. We had wild bees in our garden where I grew up and they were busy on our nearby allotment pollinating the beans and raspberries that we grew to fill the freezer for winter meals. They went about their business, flitting between the flowers and filling the air with their gentle and good vibrations. I don't remember being scared of them. I do remember being fascinated by their activity and I loved to watch them climbing right inside the bean flowers to collect their nectar supplies.

Even back then in the '70s, we pollinated the marrows and courgettes by hand, but that's because in the UK we don't have the Squash bee that has specialised in feeding on the pollen of this group of plants. But I learned fast that plants can't move around to find their perfect partner and that they need a reliable method to get pollen from one plant to another, mostly via the bees and other pollinators, sometimes by the wind and occasionally via bigger creatures such as we interfering humans.

I was and still am fascinated by plants and went on to study botany at university. Many plants can't exist without bees and the two have evolved together – perhaps that's the best way to describe how I got to where I am today. As a botanist, a love of plants comes with bees and all the other pollinators involved in their lifecycle. To be honest, these days it's the bees that turn my head more often than the flowers.

I hope you've picked this book up because you love bees and want to learn a bit more about them. More and more people are starting to understand, notice, and really care about the bees. Actually, I think it's a type of addiction, because once you get interested in these little creatures, well you just can't stop.

I am, quite honestly, addicted to bees. I'm a bee-bore, and though I still don't know everything about them, I do want to spread some bee-love and tell you more about these amazing creatures, so that you'll want to learn more too. I want to help you not just to understand the bees a little bit more, but to also do what you can to help them. When you start to learn more about these amazing creatures you realise how much you don't know, how much more there is to learn and just how intricate and fragile their existence is.

The natural balance is hanging on a precipice, not just in our seas and oceans, but on land too. The good news is that it's not too late to do something, and everyone with a garden or even just a patio, terrace or balcony can really make a difference.

What's very scary and is already happening in China is that the bees are in such dire trouble that many plants, including apple trees, are being pollinated by hand. Some hi-tech scientists are even working on building robot bees for pollination, that's quite terrifying.

We are constantly told that we have lost almost all (97 per cent) of our wildflower meadows in the UK since the Second World War. Take a moment to think about that – it means there is just 3 per cent of it left.

That's almost all the natural, wildflower forage that feeds our wild bees, and other pollinators. So it's no wonder many are in sharp decline. Rather than make AI (artificial intelligence) bees, it's time to concentrate our efforts, funding and resources on saving what we have got left.

Almost all of our wildflower meadows have been destroyed. This one is Martin Down meadow in Hampshire. © Brigit Strawbridge Howard

Honeybees are the ONLY bees that make honey in the UK. Spare a thought for the little honeybee next time you spread the honey thick and fast on your morning toast. They visit two million flowers and fly 50 000 miles to produce one pound of the amber nectar (*ref 1*). It takes twelve honeybees to make a teaspoon of honey in their lifetime. That's their winter food you are eating.

More Than Honeybees

When most people think of bees, it's usually an image of the fluffy bumblebee that fills their head, or maybe the honeybee – the little bee that collects miniscule amounts of nectar from flowers and then concentrates it into stores of honey to help it survive through the winter. When it comes to bees, the revered honeybee is just one of around 276 species of bees in the UK. Just one. And to be honest, the honeybee is probably the safest species of bee, because it has an army of beekeepers intent on keeping these bees alive and making honey. By doing whatever we can to support all bees we can make a difference. They all urgently need our love, attention and help.

We can't be precise about the exact number of bee species, because, sadly, some are on the endangered list and could go extinct at any moment; others are recent introductions and there's even one that has gone extinct in the UK and has actually been reintroduced in Kent.

Yes, we even get migrants; in the form of bees and other insects, creatures and even plants secretly arriving from abroad. Nature knows no boundaries and perhaps we could or should learn a few lessons from the way that she works.

Of those 276 bee species here in the UK, 24 or 25 are bumblebees. There really are that many different fluffy bumblebees. And the rest? Well they are rather

The Leaf-cutter bee is one of 250 different species of solitary bees in the UK. © *Jean Vernon*

unimaginatively called solitary bees and there are 250 different species of them too. And all of these bees feed on pollen and nectar and act as pollinators.

What's more, not all of the bees look like bees: some look like wasps, some look like flies and some of them are really, really tiny and you could be forgiven for not noticing them at all.

But the best bit is that they are all part of our incredible biodiversity, foraging for their survival from tiny grains of protein-rich flower pollen and energy-rich nectar and nesting in and around our gardens.

Home Help

For those who really want to help the bees, our gardens are a fantastic place to start. It's the only place where we are in control of what happens. If each and every home with a garden or even a terrace made an effort to garden with and for nature and especially for the bees, imagine what a huge difference that would make. You can start with just a pot and see what happens; it won't take long for you to realise that even just a window box full of plants can offer some food and sustenance for your local bees and other precious pollinators.

JOINING THE DOTS

Our gardens are a mosaic across the land, and bundled together make up a staggering 270,000 hectares (*Ref 2*) or 2,700 square kilometres (1,042 square miles) of privately owned garden bee reserves, where these little creatures can feed, nest and reproduce. They can be isolated pockets or they can be joined together by wildlife corridors or bee-lines that link these natural bee havens.

This book is not a text book. It's my way of sharing my love of bees and some of the bee stories I have learned along the way. It's to introduce you to some of the bees that you will find in your garden and tell you little stories about what they get up to and what makes them unique.

Acknowledgements

This book would not have been possible without the help and support of many, many people.

Martin Mulchinock my husband, who has had to chauffeur me to far flung corners of the UK to attend courses, training days and bee hunts and suffer me disappearing off on bee quests at very short notice. He created the little bee icon on each page of this book and some of the lovely photographs in this book are his too. He has endured weeks of peaks and troughs in my stress levels and hours of me being a bee-bore – thank you.

Jonathan Wright (publisher), who responded with such grace when my reply to 'Would you like to write a book about bees?' was at best rude (I didn't know who he was and I thought he was joking). He wasn't and here it is.

Bee enthusiast Brigit Strawbridge Howard, who introduced me to countless wild bees, bee experts and bee sites and offered her expertise and support at every stage without hesitation. Thanks also for allowing me to use some of her wonderful bee images and for her beautiful foreword to my first book.

Naturalist Steven Falk, who suffered my 'slow to catch on' approach to bee ID and endured my attendance at several of his bee talks, bee courses and bee walks. Always a support on Twitter and the source of the most incredible archive of bee information, bee images and of course the author of the most amazing bee book published this century, *The Field Guide to the Bees of Great Britain and Ireland*. His incredible Flickr site online is an invaluable resource for all who dabble in the dark art of bee identification. Some of his beautiful images are in this book.

Entomologist Liam Olds, who stepped in to offer further bee identification skills and technical support when I reached the sheer panic stage of a looming deadline. His calm and hugely supportive and expert advice was quite simply heaven sent. And thank you to Liam for allowing me to use some of his amazing photographs.

And a big thank you to my lovely niece, Beth Dines, for her very fresh eyed and down to earth look at and feedback on my first draft.

CHAPTER ONE

The Bees

All For One and One For All

What would you say if I told you that behind the pretty, fluffy, bug-eyed persona of your garden bees was a secret world filled with single mothers, bee imposters, theft and daylight robbery, cold blooded murder, marauding gangs, forced surrogacy and even exploding genitalia?

A White-tailed bumblebee queen (Bombus Lucorum agg) feeding on grape hyacinths in early spring. © Jean Vernon

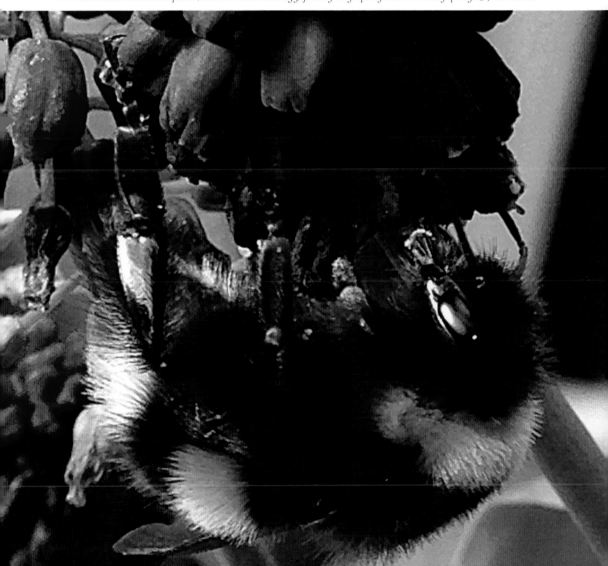

Dramatic? Well perhaps, but there's a lot more to our garden bees than meets the eye. The secret world of garden bees is complex, fascinating and truly extraordinary.

This book explores and reveals some of the fascinating behaviour of bees that you may find in your garden and shows you how to support and assist them in the hostile environment that now exists outside.

WHAT IS A BEE?

Welcome to the secret world of bees. It's a big place so let's start with explaining what a bee is.

It's complicated and if you really want an in-depth explanation, you are going to have to read a few more books. But we can at least work out what makes a bee a bee and start to understand the difference between a bee and a wasp and a fly.

It's not that simple, because in the UK there are about 276 species of bee, 7,700 species of wasp and 7,000 species of fly (including hoverflies, of which there are around 280 species). Just think about that for a moment. That's just in the UK (not the world) with all this amazing diversity across the mainland, islands and highlands.

They may all visit flowers during their lifecycle and many of them are pollinators. But just because an insect visits a flower, it doesn't make it a pollinator.

Then it gets very complicated, because some bees look like wasps, some hoverflies look like bees and some wasps look like hoverflies.

But to keep things as simple as possible, here are the basics. Do bear in mind there are always exceptions.

Wasp feeding on angelica flower head. © *Martin Mulchinock*

Some of the nomad bees like Nomada fucata *look like wasps.* © *Liam Olds*

Bees are highly complex and diverse creatures. They are insects and belong to a group of insects called Hymenoptera (ants, sawflies and some wasps are also in this group).

Bees evolved from 'meat eating' wasps sometime back in the Cretaceous period, around 100 million years ago.

While insect hunting was the usual source of protein for these early hunting insects, at some stage these creatures discovered that pollen was a good alternative to live prey, partly because it took less effort to 'catch' and also because it was very rich in protein. The rest as they say is history, and over the millennia bees have evolved into vegetarian, pollen-eating creatures in a quite close relationships with many of their food plants.

But just to confuse you, there are also some bees that really do look like wasps, mainly the nomad bees.

Don't forget that bees evolved from wasps. Wasps, of which there are 7,700 UK species, including the social wasps that arrive uninvited to our summer picnics, lunches and parties, feed their offspring a rich diet of caterpillars, aphids and other insect prey, while the adults devour nectar and pollen just like the bees.

BEE MIMICS
There are many other creatures that mimic the bees to save themselves from being eaten by predators. They take on the stripy look of a stinging bee to give themselves a head start against attack. A second's delay in a predator deciding whether they are a bee or a tasty snack can give them precious moments to escape.

Body Language

So how do you tell a bee from a fly or a wasp? After all they are all insects with three main parts to their bodies; a head (top), a thorax (middle) and an abdomen (bottom).

- Bees have two pairs of wings. The second pair is smaller and sometimes hard to see, but look closely, and if there are four wings then it s a bee.
- When stationary, bees wings tend to be folded back onto the body, whereas fly wings are more aeroplane-like and at an angle to the body (but not always!).
- Bees have quite large eyes on the sides of their heads. Flies have very large eyes that are on the front of the head and tend to join in the middle.
- Bees are usually hairy or fuzzy whereas wasps and most flies are usually not.
- Bees have a waist and longer antennae.

BEE

ANTENNAE: LONGER

EYES: SIDE OF HEAD

HEAD

THORAX

WINGS: TWO PAIRS

WAIST: BEES HAVE A WAIST

HAIRY: BEES ARE HAIRY

© Liam Olds

ABDOMEN

- Flies have short stumpy antennae that are sometimes hard to see.
- Bees are vegetarian and collect pollen. So anything carrying a pollen load is a bee. But remember that flies can have a dusting of pollen on their bodies.
- Social wasps (those black and yellow rather annoying insects that pester us on our summer picnics) drink nectar and eat pollen, but they also collect other insects such as aphids and caterpillars to feed their larvae.
- Most bees and some wasps can sting, but flies can't. Solitary bee 'stings' are weak and usually undetectable.
- It's the females of the species that sting; that's because their egg-laying apparatus has evolved to enable them to inject venom into prey, but it is also as a defence. Male bees don't have the same physical attributes but some have spiky pointy bottoms that can be used to prick in self-defence.
- Wasps, bees and even flies all visit flowers and many of them are excellent pollinators. They visit flowers for their nectar and pollen.

FLY

ANTENNAE: SHORT & STUMPY

EYES: LARGER & ON TOP

HEAD

THORAX

WINGS: ONE PAIR

WAIST: FLIES DON'T HAVE A WAIST

HAIRY: FLIES ARE LESS HAIRY

ABDOMEN

Hoverfly © Liam Olds

TO BEE OR NOT TOO BEE

Not only are there bees that don't really look like bees, but also there are many creatures that have an uncanny resemblance to bees and for different reasons. Remember, just because it looks like a bee doesn't mean it is a bee and you might be surprised at the mimicry that exists in nature.

Bee Flies

These fluffy little insects are as hairy as a bumblebee; that's unusual for a fly. They dart around the flowers too, just like a bee, with a proboscis sticking out ready to sup nectar. Bee flies (*Bombylius major*) are the size of a small bumblebee and on the wing in spring.

*Look out for the Bee fly (*Bombylius major*) in spring. © Liam Olds*

But these are bee flies, flies that look like bees. And they are bee parasites, flicking their eggs into solitary bee nests as they fly past, where they hatch, feed on the food provided by the mother bee and starve out the bee larvae, in effect taking over the nest. It's a bit harsh if your passion is for bees, but these little insects have their place in the ecosystem, and where they are thriving you can be sure that your solitary bee species are too.

Drone Flies

There is a whole group of hoverflies that look remarkably like a male honeybee, called a drone, and are aptly known as a drone flies. *Eristalis tenax* is the scientific name for one of these and it is a very common insect in our UK gardens. Look closely and you will see that it has large insect eyes like a fly, because it is a fly and it only has one set of wings. These insects can hover mid air and just like bees they feed on the nectar of flowers.

The Common drone fly (Eristalis tenax) looks like a male honeybee. © Martin Mulchinock

Cuckoo Bumblebees

Cuckoo bumblebees are real bees and they have an uncanny knack of looking just like the bee species that they affect.

Just like their namesake, the cuckoo, these bees lay their eggs in their host bee's nest and cuckold the host bees, so that they raise the cuckoo bee's young. There are several species of cuckoo bumblebees that you may find in your garden, which parasitise specific species of bumblebee.

Solitary bees also have cuckoo bee species that parasitise their nests, but unlike the bumblebee cuckoos they don't generally look like their hosts. So for example some of

Both these bumblebees are male. The bee on the left is the Early bumblebee (Bombus pratorum) *which is the host species of the cuckoo bee* (Bombus sylvestris) *on the right.* © Jean Vernon

the nomad bees, of which there are around 30 UK species, lay their eggs in the nests of some of the mining bees (*Andrena*), and their larvae feed on the food provided for each egg by the solitary bee host.

GARDEN BEES

Bees know no boundaries. Just like all wildlife they move from fast food outlets in the hedgerows and fields into our gardens with no comprehension of the boundaries we have tattooed on the land. In built up areas it is the presence of gardens, waste ground and even road verges and roundabouts that support these precious creatures, and yet if we joined each patch together like a giant virtual jigsaw, the area of just our private gardens alone would in effect be a vast 270,000 hectare nature reserve. Each and every garden can make a difference.

To help the bees we need to start with our gardens and work outwards.

For the bees to prosper and thrive we need to set our own garden rules, be aware of the dangers facing bees of all types and have a future-proof plan for all pollinators. Most of all we need an understanding of their lifecycle, their needs and their quirky behaviour so that we can keep them safe and share the beauty and idiosyncrasies of bees with others and spread the love.

Our gardens are a vital habitat for most species of bees. © Martin Mulchinock/Tom Burns

Dangerous World

The bee world is not always the cute and fluffy place that we would like to think. These creatures are not just contending with the toxic landscape that man has created, but they have their own extraordinary hurdles to jump, in their race to simply survive and continue their species. We've thrown a lot of curve balls at nature in the last century but the bees have plenty of other things to overcome to ensure their survival. Ten per cent of wild bees are facing extinction. In recent memory three UK bumblebees have become extinct.

Bees could be considered to be the canary in the coalmine. These sensitive creatures are telling us something and we need to listen. Since the 1930s we have lost almost all of our wildflower meadows (97 per cent), and we have changed the landscape dramatically, depriving bees (and many other creatures) of precious nesting and feeding habitat. Add to the mix the rising use of highly toxic pesticides, urbanisation and climate change and you start to understand the real pressures that our bees and all other creatures are facing.

CHAPTER TWO

Meet the Bees

Bee world is generally a selfless society. The social bees, as we call them, those that form a colony and include the bumblebees and the honeybee, live an altruistic life, totally focused on the good of the colony and doing whatever is needed to ensure the survival of the whole community.

GARDEN BUMBLEBEES

Of the 25 species of bumblebees in the UK, just seven or eight of them are considered to be common and these are the ones that you are most likely to see in your garden. Learning the difference between these bees is fun and although it can be a little complicated, it is well worth the effort. The best way to grasp the basics is to join a bumblebee identification (ID) course, a bee safari or a bee walk. These are run regularly through spring and summer by the Bumblebee Conservation Trust (*Ref 3*). The Trust also publishes a great little book on bumblebees and several bee ID posters, pocket guides and cheat sheets, which are well worth keeping close by. Take photographs and use the online ID guides, such as *Blooms for Bees*, which are widely available. But as with most things practice makes perfect.

The Garden Bumblebee (*Bombus hortorum*)

Gardeners should be very honoured because we actually have our very own garden bumblebee that is commonly known as just that, the Garden bumblebee, with the scientific name of *Bombus hortorum* (*ref 4*). Of all the bumblebees this one is one of the easiest species to identify because it has a long, narrow head (hortorum – think horse, though of course it's the horticulture bee!), otherwise it is quite similar in its colouring to some other fairly common bumblebees, like the White-tailed bumblebee (*Bombus lucorum*). The Garden bumblebees have the longest tongues (up to around 1.5cm in length, though it can be longer) which enables them to feed from deep flowers such as foxgloves, comfrey and vetches, and when flying from flower to flower they often leave their tongue extended so they look like sword-bees or unicorns. When not extended the tongue is usually folded under their head and thorax.

The Garden bumblebee keeps its tongue hanging out as it moves from flower to flower. © Jean Vernon

While the Garden bumblebee does resemble the buff and white-tailed species, the main differences are that these bees are slimmer, have a longer head and they have two bands of yellow hairs on the thorax (think back pack) and three yellow bands in total. There is another bumblebee that has similar triple yellow stripes but a shorter, blunter face, called the Heath bumblebee (*Bombus jonellus*), which despite its name, can be found in gardens.

The Garden bumblebee makes surface or shallow nests in the garden. This is the bee that will also choose very odd places to nest. I once had one try and build a nest under my pillow and I know another bee enthusiast had a similar experience with a bee nesting under a duvet. Reports of coat pockets and inside lawnmowers (*Ref 5*) are also known.

The Garden bumblebee nests are relatively small compared to other species, with perhaps 100–150 bees at the peak, and the nests are short lived, around 3–4 months at a time.

How to spot

Stake out some of the flowers in your garden that this bee feeds on. Large flowers are popular. Bees foraging on foxgloves are almost invariably this species.

Look out for the narrower body, the long tongue sticking out as the bee flies, its triple yellow stripes, the third one right at the base of the thorax, and the longer head, all unusual features of the species which set it apart from others, although the much rarer Ruderal bumblebee (*Bombus ruderatus*) looks very similar.

Cuckoo bee – the Garden bumblebee's nest can be taken over by the Barbut's cuckoo bee (*Bombus barbutellus*).

The cage-like flowers of garden acanthus can trap the Garden bumblebee as it tries to access the nectar. © *Jean Vernon*

How to help

Grow some flowers that this species loves such as viper's bugloss (*Echium vulgare*), lavender, foxgloves and other long tubular flowers like penstemons, comfrey, salvias and members of the pea family, including the vetches and bird's foot trefoil.

Cut off the flowering spikes of acanthus plants, as the Garden bumblebees can climb inside the flowers attracted by the nectar flow and become trapped, where they die. Late emerging queen Garden bumblebees caught in this way will deprive your garden of a whole generation of bees.

The Tree Bumblebee (*Bombus hypnorum*)

The Tree bumblebee is actually a relative newcomer to the British Isles, first appearing here in 2001. It's a bee that you may have had first hand experience of as it is common in gardens and often makes nests under house eaves or in garden bird boxes, and like its name suggests, also in holes in trees. It's a social bee forming small colonies of bees and these nests can get quite busy. In fact, they are so busy that many people mistake their presence for a swarm and get quite worried about them. Usually this is around mid to late summer when the nests get surrounded by rather keen male bees waiting for the freshly hatched queen bees to emerge.

It's an early emerging bumblebee, with the overwintering queens first appearing as the weather starts to warm from February onwards, and quite unusually for

bumblebees they search vertically for a suitable nest site, perhaps the reason why they choose to nest up high. Bird boxes provide the perfect size nest space for these buoyant little bees. An established nest can contain as many as 150 bees, and by mid summer, when the colony's new queens have hatched and emerged, the attention from the hopeful male bees looking to mate can create a real buzz around the nest. In a similar way if the nest is disturbed, feisty bees can boil out of the nest and sting anyone nearby. This behaviour has given the Tree bumblebee a bit of a reputation for being aggressive.

The lovely Tree bumblebee is a relative newcomer to the UK. © Jean Vernon

How to spot

If you've got a bumblebee nest in a garden bird box or under the house eaves it's more than likely to be a colony of Tree bumblebees. These bees are quite distinctive with a chestnut orange red back pack (thorax), black abdomen and a white tip to their tails.

Cuckoo bee – the Tree bumblebee doesn't seem to have a cuckoo bee species that affects it in the UK, but in Europe its cuckoo bee is *Bombus norvegicus*.

How to help

Plant plenty of spring and summer flowering plants, not forgetting plants that are in flower in late winter and autumn too. Tree bumblebees have shorter tongues so need flowers that have short corollas and where the pollen and nectar is accessible. Think daisies, thistles, coneflowers, blackberries and raspberries.

Leave one used nest box for the Tree bumblebees. Site it away from the house where it won't cause any concerns, about 3 metres high in a secure and stable place. It might be taken over by a nesting bird or it could provide the perfect site for a Tree bumblebee nest.

The Buff-Tailed Bumblebee (*Bombus terrestris*)

In early spring when out in your garden, look out for these fluffy flying golf balls whizzing around the garden searching for nectar and pollen. They are loud and large and pretty unmistakable. These are the queens of this beautiful bumblebee and they are some of the largest bumblebees you will see in your garden. The Buff-tailed bumblebee is a common, widespread garden species and can even be present in some more southerly gardens all year round, even in winter, due to winter active second colonies. The large queens emerge from their winter cavity early in February in favourable conditions and will feed on a wide variety of garden plants. It's pretty

Buff-tailed bumblebee on verbena bonariensis. © Martin Mulchinock

much only the queens that have the buffish beige tail tip; the workers and the males of this species have white bottoms which makes them difficult to distinguish from the White-tailed bumblebees. Even the experts struggle.

The Buff-tailed bumblebee has a short tongue but this doesn't restrict it to feeding on just open accessible and short corolla flowers, because it has learnt to rob long tubular flowers by chewing holes above the nectary on the flowers.

This bee nests in old vole and mouse holes, usually underground (hence its scientific name *terrestris* – meaning of the earth/land) and is also known to make nests under garden sheds and in compost heaps/bins. The nests are among the largest of the bumblebees and at their peak may contain 400 bees.

How to spot
The workers of this bee can be difficult to distinguish from the White-tailed bumblebee. It is the queens that are the easiest to identify as they have a buffish beige tail and orangey yellow bands on the thorax. You can spot these bees feeding on your garden flowers, especially those with short flowers or very open, accessible flowers where the bees can reach the nectar and pollen easily.

The queens have a lot of work to do to provision the nest and feed the very first brood, so they tend to forage fairly close to their nests. Winter active bumblebees are often the Buff-tailed bumblebee; this species can be found nesting from autumn until spring and will appreciate winter flowering trees and shrubs in the garden.

Cuckoo bee – The Buff-tailed bumblebee is a host for the similar looking Southern cuckoo bee (*Bombus vestalis*).

How to help
Grow lots of flowers in your garden that have accessible pollen and nectar. Especially early flowering plants that are a bee lifesaver in late winter and early spring, such as heathers and mahonia. Remember that the queens of this species are big and quite heavy so they need strong-stemmed flowers with easy access nectar and pollen, or landing pads where they can descend and feed safely on flowers that will support their weight, such as scabious, lavender, roses and marigolds or cushion plants such as thyme.

Plant a bee shrub or tree or two that will establish in time to bear hundreds of flowers in one small area; a willow tree or an open flowered cherry is a good choice.

Grow a wide variety of plants and flowers to give your wild bees a decent choice of forage plants. Let the dandelions and thistles flower. Any flowers with a flat, central disc, such as daisies, cosmos, and coneflowers are ideal as they offer a landing pad for the bees, while the central disc is actually made up of dozens of tiny floral tubes that the bees can easily feed from.

Don't spray your garden or your plants with pesticides of any sort. Anything designed to kill insects will also kill bees, even organic pest controls. Remove pests by

The Southern cuckoo bee resembles its host and feeds on similar flowers. © Jean Vernon

hand where possible and if necessary. For an aphid attack wash plants with a jet of water that blasts the aphids to the ground for the ground feeding birds to eat.

Encourage wildlife into the garden as natural pest control.

Keep a watch out for bumblebee nests in your garden and if there's one present protect it so that pets, children and other garden visitors don't interfere with it.

White-Tailed Bumblebee (*Bombus lucorum agg*)

The queen bees of the White-tailed bumblebee, like the Buff-tailed are also early emerging, large bees. With white tails and more lemony yellow bands on the thorax, it is another common garden bumblebee and one that you will find feeding on your garden plants. It's been fairly recently discovered that there are actually three forms of this species in the UK, though you will be pretty unlikely to tell them apart by sight. Experts use DNA testing to distinguish between *Bombus lucorum* and the similar sub species *Bombus cryptarum* and *Bombus magnus*. Currently any sightings are denoted as being *Bombus lucorum agg* (agg meaning aggregate).

It's another short-tongued species favouring flowers with accessible nectar and pollen. They are also nectar robbers and will bite holes in the base of flowers such as comfrey, salvias and other longer tubular flowers and soak up nectar through these holes, because their tongues are too short to actually reach the nectar. It's a very clever adaptation and doesn't seem to affect the efficacy of pollination of the plants in general. These bees also nest in old rodent nests, such as mouse and vole holes.

How to spot

If you've got a garden you are very likely to see these bees feeding on your flowers.

The yellow banding on these bees is more lemony yellow than the dirty yellow of the Buff-tailed bumblebees.

Look out for the White-tailed queen bees in early spring feeding on flowers or zigzagging low over the ground surveying for suitable nest sites.

Once the workers emerge in early summer it's pretty difficult to tell these bees apart from workers of the Buff-tailed bumblebee. White-tailed worker bees are not all *Bombus lucorum*.

Look out for bees nectar robbing and feeding on garden flowers and do your best to identify them using photography.

Cuckoo bee – the White-tailed bumblebee is parasitised by the Gypsy cuckoo bee (*Bombus bohemicus*).

How to help

Anything you can do in your garden to help bees will support this species. It has very similar needs to most other bumblebees in terms of nesting sites, forage and protection. Plant more flowers, avoid pesticides and let the lawn flower.

  THE SECRET LIVES OF GARDEN BEES

The queen White-tailed bumblebees look similar to the Buff-tailed queens, but usually have brighter yellow bands. © Martin Mulchinock

The Gypsy cuckoo bee is a parasite of the White-tailed bumblebee. © BBCT/Kim Berry

Think bees when choosing plants to grow in your garden. Choose plants with single flowers where the pollen and nectaries are exposed. Plant more. The queens of this species are too big and too heavy to delicately cling to small flowers, and need strong stemmed flowers with easy access to nectar and pollen, or landing pads where they can descend and feed safely on flowers that will support their weight, such as knapweeds and thistles.

Let the lawn grow longer and allow the daisies and clover to flower.

Leave a section of the lawn to flower and plant more wildflowers into this area using special native wildflower plug plants.

Thistles of all types are fabulous bee plants. This knapweed is packed with pollen and nectar. © Jean Vernon

The Red-Tailed Bumblebee (*Bombus lapidarius*)

This dark beautiful bumblebee has a rich orange red tail making it one of the easiest bees to identify. The queen bees and workers are mostly black with a distinctive red bottom. It is widespread across the UK and a common bee that you will find in parks and gardens, foraging on flowers. It has been suggested that this bee has a preference for yellow flowers (*Ref 6*). It is another short-tongued bumblebee that will feed on plants where the flower head is made up of many individual flowers.

The queen bees emerge in March and April and will nest in old rodent holes and also in stone walls. The first workers to emerge can be very small and will set to work collecting pollen and nectar for the next generations. The male bees have the distinctive red bottom and yellow facial hair and also a yellow thorax.

There is a similar looking, but much rarer bumblebee called the Red-shanked carder bee (*Bombus ruderarius*), which has orange hairs on its hind legs.

Cuckoo bee – the aptly named Red-tailed cuckoo bee (*Bombus rupestris*) uses the Red-tailed bumblebee as its host.

It's easy to tell the male Bombus lapidarius *by his big red bottom and yellow thorax.* © *Jean Vernon*

The Red-tailed cuckoo bee (Bombus rupestris) infiltrates the nests of the Red-tailed bumblebee looks similar, with a rich red bottom. © Jean Vernon

How to spot

This is a common garden bee, but will also be found out in the wider landscape/countryside. Look out for it in public gardens and parks; it's very easy to identify and though there is a much rarer bumblebee it could be confused with, this is unlikely.

Look out for these long black bees with distinctive red bottoms on garden flowers. Does it seem to prefer yellow flowers in your garden, or do you find it feasting on something different?

How to help

Let the wildflowers in the lawn grow and flower. This bee will feed on bird's foot trefoil, dandelions, thistles and daisies. Whatever you do to help the bees in general will benefit this species.

Leave north facing banks undisturbed from late summer until spring; these are the preferred spots for the overwintering queens of this species. If you are observant or have ever accidentally dug up an overwintering Red-tailed bumblebee, then make a note of where it was, as these bees are known to overwinter in these sites year after year. (*Ref 7*)

The Common Carder Bee (*Bombus pascuorum*)

These lovely little bumblebees are common in gardens and feed on our garden flowers with great enthusiasm. They often have quite stripy bottoms and are one of four bumblebee species sometimes referred to as the ginger bees. The Common carder bee is a beautiful little creature with a ginger, chestnut orange backpack (thorax) and a ginger and black stripy looking abdomen and tail. These bees are widespread in the countryside, foraging on the flowers growing in pasture and verges, or anywhere that the flowers grow.

There are also two other rarer carder bees that look similar, the Brown-banded carder bee (*Bombus humilis*) and the Moss carder bee (*Bombus muscorum*) and one very rare carder bee called the Shrill carder bee (*Bombus sylvarum*), which unless you visit the few hotspots in south Wales, Thames Estuary and Somerset, you are pretty unlikely to see.

The male Common carder bee has ginger facial hair. The queens emerge in March and visit a wide variety of flowers, collecting pollen and nectar from those with longer corollas because they have a medium length tongue and can access deeper nectaries. (*Ref 8*)

They will also climb into complex flowers such as snap dragons (antirrhinums), sweetpeas and the oft-dreaded Himalayan balsam.

These bees make shallow nests, often at ground level or in tussocky grass, and are known to cover the nest with moss and dried grass.

As these bees age they can become very faded and worn and can look quite different to a newly emerged bee, making identification tricky and complicated.

These bees are active for the longest period and can be found in and around gardens right into autumn.

The Common carder bee has a long tongue and needs a range of plants where it can access the deeper nectaries. © Jean Vernon

The Common carder bee makes a shallow nest and loosely weaves moss and dried grass to camouflage it. © BBCT/ Raymond Hutcheon

How to spot

If you have bumblebees in your garden you are more than likely to have this bee foraging and nesting nearby. It's possibly the most common bumblebee in our gardens.

Look out for gingery stripy bees, check the tail and if it's not white then you've probably got the Common carder bee. Enjoy their enthusiastic foraging.

How to help

Grow a rich diversity of flowers in your garden, especially simple, open flowers and early flowers like comfrey.

Leave moss to grow in part of your lawn.

Allow a little of your garden to go or stay wild. Let the dandelions flower.

Grow antirrhinums, clovers and vetches to support wild bees.

Let the flowers keep flowering, encouraging later flowering by using the Chelsea chop and cutting back borders late in the season to leave forage for these late active bees. If you have a meadow, don't cut it in midsummer, or at least leave a third of it to finish flowering so that you protect any nest sites and leave forage for these bees.

The Early Bumblebee (*Bombus pratorum*)

Just as its name suggests, the Early bumblebee is one of the first to emerge and nest in spring. The queen bees are smaller than the other early emerging queens such as *Bombus terrestris* and *Bombus lucorum*.

It's a fast little bee that can be found in the garden feeding on spring beauties such as flowering currants (ribes), primulas and grape hyacinths (muscari).

It's a black and yellow-banded bumblebee and the telltale give away for identification for the queen bees, the males and the worker bees, is the little red orange tip to the tail. Compared to the Red-tailed bumblebee, which is black with a larger splash of red orange on its bottom, the red hairs on the Early bumblebee tail are just at the tip.

The Early bumblebee has a short tongue, like the other early emergers, and so feeds on smaller flowers like wallflowers, open flowers such as hardy geraniums (cranesbill) and complex flowers where there are many flowers together in one place, such as thistles, dandelions and daisies.

Cuckoo bee – the Early bumblebee nest can be taken over by the Forest cuckoo bee (*Bombus sylvestris*). This is one of the most common cuckoo bumblebees in the UK.

The Early bumblebee can be a host to the Forest cuckoo bee Bombus sylvestris. @ BBCT/Nick Owens

How to spot

Look around the garden flowers in February and March for the Early bumblebee queens. These are small compared to the other early emergers. Look at the tail tip as it's a good indicator of species: this bee has an orange-red tip to the very end of its tail. In my garden it's commonly seen on flowering currants and the perennial borage (*Trachystemon orientalis*). But it can and will take advantage of robbing holes made by the Buff and White-tailed bumblebees.

How to help

Grow more early flowering plants that will be in bloom when the queens emerge in spring. This is the critical period for these bees. They won't fly too far from their nest to gather food, so if you see them in the garden then they are nesting nearby. Look out for the males in late spring feeding on your garden plants.

Avoid plants that have been treated with pesticides to ensure your bees don't take a dose of poison with the nectar and pollen and concentrate it back at the nest.

Plant soft fruit such as currants, raspberries and blackberries – food for the bees and fruit for you.

The Early bumblebees may carry out secondary robbing where holes have been made to steal nectar from flowers with longer corollas, like this comfrey. © Jean Vernon

SPECIALIST GARDEN BUMBLEBEES

There are actually 25 species of bumblebees recorded in the UK and some of them are very rare. Each bee species has a story but often for the rarer ones it's a tale of specialisation, isolation or devastation. Fortunately there are several projects ongoing that are not just recording the last strongholds of these bees, but doing really constructive work to improve the habitat and floral bounty of the areas where they are clinging on.

The Great Yellow Bumblebee (*Bombus distinguendus*)

This golden treasure is one of the rarest bees in the UK.

You are not going to see the Great yellow bumblebee (*Ref 9 and Ref 10*) in your garden. But you do need to know about it, it's the largest bumblebee in the British Isles and one of the most dramatic looking too. It's big and yellow and stripy and was once widespread across the British Isles. These days it can only be found in the far reaches of Britain in the flower rich Scottish highlands and islands. It feeds predominantly on bird's foot trefoil (*Lotus corniculatus*) in spring and as the season matures it then feeds on red clover and knapweeds.

The Great yellow bumblebee was once widespread across the UK. Today it survives in the extremities of Scotland. © Brigit Strawbridge Howard

For a big bee it has a surprisingly small colony of around 80 or so bees, so the production of daughter queen bees to carry the species forward may be limited in each nest. These bees nest in tussocky maram grass and also in disused rodent and rabbit holes. They emerge quite late in spring, around May time.

Cuckoo bee – because the Great yellow bumblebee is now so isolated, its populations do not overlap with any known cuckoo bee species, though it has been suggested that the Field cuckoo bee may once have predated on this rare bee species.

How to spot
You are going to have to travel to see this bee, right up to the Scottish islands or across into Ireland. Then seek out a valley rich in bird's foot trefoil, red clover and knapweed and you might be lucky.

How to help
There's not much that you can do in your own garden to support this rare bee, but that doesn't mean you can't help some of the others.

Let the clover and other wildflowers grow in part of your lawn.

Cut the lawn in stages, leaving one third to grow longer and flower for a few weeks.

Plant wildflowers in your lawns and flower borders. Not all good bee plants are wildflowers or native. Always avoid tightly packed petals, double flowers and highly bred varieties, instead choosing open flowers, single flowers and scented forms where the nectar and pollen is accessible.

Stop using all types of pesticides and try to garden using organic principles.

Grow from seed and cuttings or buy plants from nurseries that are either organic or that don't treat the plants with chemicals.

Bilberry Bumblebee (*Bombus monticola*)

The Bilberry bumblebee (*Ref 11, 12, 13*) is more commonly found in northern and western Britain and occurs now in upland areas at an altitude above 300m in Wales, northern England and Scotland. It's now considered to be a rare bee in some areas and is currently the subject of a project by the Bumblebee Conservation Trust called 'Pollinating the Peak'. It prefers upland and moorland but has also been recorded at sea level in Scotland, northern England and Wales. It is also known as the Mountain bumblebee due to its distribution, or the Blaeberry bumblebee because it feeds on bilberries. Like many of the rarer species it is a fairly specialised feeder and it's a long tongued bumblebee too.

Where they are grown as a commercial crop, blueberries, which are closely related to bilberries, are commonly pollinated by bumblebees. In fact their shrubby, gnarled and woody stems and roots create the perfect nesting site for mice and voles and it is often the old abandoned rodent holes that provide the perfect nest site for newly

This pretty, but rare, Bilberry bumblebee is part of a conservation project, designed to support its last remaining populations. © BBCT/Anne Riley

emerged mated queen bumblebees; the resulting nests and colonies are thus perfectly placed to effect excellent pollination of the crop.

The queens of the Bilberry bumblebee emerge in April and nest under vegetation or sometimes just under the soil surface. They often nest in old rodent holes and may well have evolved alongside the bilberry plants on which they feed, nesting between the roots. The queen bees will collect the pollen from a wide range of plants including the bilberries, but also willows, clovers and brambles as well as raspberries and bird's foot trefoil.

Nests are usually relatively small with approximately 50 or so workers. These bees are quite distinctive with a rich orange red abdomen and a bright yellow band at the top of the thorax.

Cuckoo bee – The Bilberry bumblebee is a host species for the Forest cuckoo bee (*Bombus sylvestris*).

Bilberry bumblebee nests can be taken over by the Forest cuckoo bumblebee. © BBCT/Dawn Ewing

How to spot

Look out for this bee where the bilberries grow wild. It's a rare bumblebee that is not widely distributed so unless you garden near its pockets of distribution you are unlikely to see it in and around your garden. Consider it as a rare treasure and one that's worth seeking out, especially if you travel to northern or western counties where it is recorded.

How to help

Plant blueberries and cranberries into pots of ericaceous compost. These are great food plants for all types of bees and will help support your local bee population whether you have the Bilberry bumblebee near you or not. And you get the added and excellent bonus of a steady trickle of ripened berries to add to your morning breakfast cereal.

If you find this bee take photographs, confirm your identification skills and share your record with the Bees, Wasps and Ants Recording Society (BWARS).

The Short-Haired Bumblebee (*Bombus subterraneus*)

There's a quite fascinating story surrounding this rare bumblebee species, which is eloquently told in Dave Goulson's book, *A Sting in the Tale*. (*Ref 15*).

The Short-haired bumblebee (*Ref 14*) is (or perhaps was) one of our UK native bees and it was once widespread. Like many bees its population went into decline after the Second World War and very sadly this species was last recorded in the UK in 1988. In 2000 it was actually declared to be extinct in the UK. But the bee does still exist in New Zealand where the current bees are actually modern generations of the same species that were exported to New Zealand in the late nineteenth century to pollinate the red clover that is such an important crop there. The bees established there quite successfully, taking advantage of the swathes of red clover and flower-rich habitat.

In recent years a joint initiative between several NGOs looked into reintroducing the species from New Zealand back to the UK, but the seasonal differences and the genetic diversity of the population there threw doubts upon the plan. After much consideration, it was decided that there was a stronger population of this species in Sweden and that the climate there was similar to the reintroduction site in the UK; both essential decision making factors. A huge number of checks were made to ensure that there would be minimal impact on the Swedish population and that the 'new' bees wouldn't introduce any pests or diseases back to the wild bees in the UK.

Red clover is an excellent bee plant and a perfect source of nectar for long-tongued bees like the Short-haired bumblebee. © BBCT/Dave Goulson

Eventually healthy queen Short-haired bumblebees were collected, health checked and quarantined and finally, with much excitement, fifty queens were released into the RSPB Dungeness nature reserve, in Kent, in 2012.

Remember that the queen bees mate quickly after they emerge and are then ready and able to make a nest and start a colony, bringing with them the genetics of the NZ male bumblebee that they have mated with to the UK, to widen the genetic diversity of any potential new colony. Further queen bees have been released over recent years and worker caste Short-haired bumblebees have been recorded in the area. This means that some of the queen bees have raised a brood and worker bees, indicating some degree of success. It's a waiting game now to see whether there really is a population building in the area. Regular bee recording sessions and experts trained to identify this species are keeping a close watch for signs of success. The hope is to bring this bee back from the brink of extinction.

One of the key and additional success stories of the project is the huge improvement of flower rich habitat in the area, not just in quantity but in quality too. Suitable habitat creation has been a vital part of the project and has had a very encouraging effect on other bumblebee species, some of which have been recorded at the reserve after gaps of 10 and up to 40 years. It's a very exciting project that is supported by a number of volunteers who record bumblebee species and help with other aspects of the scheme.

Even rare bumblebees usually have a cuckoo bee associated with them. The Barbut's cuckoo bee is thought to lay its eggs in the nest of the Short-haired bumblebee. © BBCT/Graham White

It is now in Phase 2, which aims to continue to improve the flower rich forage for all bees in the area and to monitor and record all of the rare bumblebees, including the Short-haired bumblebee. It's a work in progress and developments and news are emerging regularly; keep up to date on social media and by visiting the project's website (*Ref 16*).

Cuckoo bee – this rare bumblebee is thought to be a host for the Barbut's cuckoo bee (*Bombus barbutellus*).

How to spot

The Short-haired bumblebee is only going to be found in and around the Romney Marshes and Dungeness in Kent and then only if you are very lucky. If you want to see this bee then your best bet is to join in with some of the events, activities and volunteering opportunities with the Bumblebee Conservation Trust.

The bees aren't very easy to distinguish from other bumblebees so you are better getting advice from bee experts working on the project.

How to help

Get involved in the project by volunteering and attending events. Learn more about this rare bee and other bumblebees and plant flowers suitable for these longer tongued bees to feed on. The Short-haired bumblebee feeds on red clover, bird's foot trefoil and viper's bugloss. Plant these nectar rich plants wherever you can, as they will provide essential food for all other bees too.

Spread the word, shout it from the tree tops, these wild bees are vital pollinators and need every form of support we can muster. Whatever you can do to help any species of bees will have a knock on effect on the environment and help other bees and pollinators with similar food resource needs.

Read the books. Learn to identify bees and share the joy. Become a bee-bore and spread the word. Too many bees that need our help, too little time.

THE GINGER BEES

There are four bumblebees that are sometimes referred to as the ginger bees. The most common one is the Common carder bee (*Bombus pascuorum*). But there are three other ginger bumblebees you might be lucky enough to come across. These include the Brown-banded carder bee (*Bombus humilis*), the Moss carder bee (*Bombus muscorum*) and the very rare Shrill carder bee (*Bombus sylvarum*).

Brown-Banded Carder Bee (*Bombus humilis*)

This little bee is one of the brown or gingery bumblebees and quite a rare one too. Personally I have only seen it in Wales, on The Gower when it joined us on a bee identification day with the renowned bee expert Steven Falk, and more recently at the RSPB Newport Wetlands when I joined a BWARS Cymru day looking for bees.

The lovely ginger Brown-banded carder bee feeds on meadow vetchling (Lathyrus pratensis). © Jean Vernon

To the untrained eye the Brown-banded carder bee (*Ref 17 and Ref 18*) looks pretty similar to the Common carder bee to which it is closely related, and indeed to the other gingery brown carder bees. And like all these bees it can be difficult to correctly identify unless you go out with a bee expert or you really know your stuff.

The queens are perhaps the easiest caste to spot and identify, as they have a distinctive yellow-banded abdomen and a waistband of brown with a very gingery backpack (thorax). It's not a garden bee generally and if you are lucky enough to spot this bee it is more likely to be in open flower-rich areas. It's easy to confuse with the much more widespread *Bombus pascuorum*, the Common carder bee.

Cuckoo bee – this species is host for the Field cuckoo bee (*Bombus campestris*).

Special behaviour/how to spot

Go out with a bee expert in areas where this bee has been recorded. You are more likely to see the Common carder bee, but check any gingery bee using the *Blooms for Bees* app or Steven Falk's Flickr album to identify correctly. You can gently capture flying bees into a magnifying pot to examine them safely, but don't trap them for long and release them carefully where you have found them. If the bees have any black hairs (be careful because the body beneath is black so it can be hard to tell) then it is a Common carder bee.

How you can help

Leave a patch of long grass in your garden.

Don't mow down meadows and flowering grasslands in mid summer, or if you really must, leave a big section to finish flowering; these bees are late foragers and need large areas of clovers, vetches, bird's foot trefoils and thistles to flower into early autumn. (*Ref 19*)

Shrill Carder Bee (*Bombus sylvarum*)

Considered by many to be the rarest bumblebee in Britain, the Shrill carder bee (*Ref 20*) is only known in a small cluster of fragmented locations. But it is also part of a Bumblebee Conservation Trust project to preserve, conserve and protect it, and now that some of its haunts are known there is an action plan to help it re-establish and thrive. Its main strong holds are in the Thames estuary in Essex and Kent, in a few spots in Wales including Gwent Levels, Glamorganshire coast and Castlemartin Range, Pembrokeshire and at a few sites in Somerset and Wiltshire, namely the Salisbury plain and National Trust property Lytes Cary Manor and the surrounding areas.

This bee is particularly distinctive because of its colouring and its higher pitched buzz. These bees have a black stripe across their back pack (thorax) that divides a pale straw yellow band, with a reddish, orange tail and a band of black hairs between its wings. The queens emerge in April and May (and sometimes June) and are much larger than the workers and the males. It's now the focus of the Bumblebee

Conservation Trust 'Back from the Brink' project and is a UK BAP protected species (UK Biodiversity Action Plan). Work is afoot to add wildflower field margins around areas where it is found and to protect the brown field sites where it occurs.

The Shrill carder bee feeds on a variety of flowers (*Ref 22*) with its long tongue, particularly knapweed (it is also known as the Knapweed carder bee), vetches, red clover, deadnettles, hedge woundwort, black horehound, meadow vetchling and red bartsia.

Special behaviour/how to spot

You are going to need to seek out this bee in order to see it, but there are plenty of projects supporting it that are in need of volunteers and recorders. If you are lucky enough to see this rare bee, the main behaviour you are likely to observe is its slightly higher pitched buzz. Go out with some bee experts to some of its known locations. It's a similar size and shape to other carder bees and can be tricky to tell apart, but it is a paler straw yellow in colour and has a distinctive orange tail.

Cuckoo bee – none known.

Another rare bee with a long tongue, the Shrill carder bee feeds on red clover, vetches and knapweeds. © BBCT

How you can help

Join the Bumblebee Conservation Trust and support its conservation work. Become a volunteer and get involved with the Somerset Shrill Carder Group or the 'Back from the Brink' project for this endangered bee.

Grow flowers for long tongued bumblebees, as this will help other wild bees in your neighbourhood.

Encourage neighbours, schools and councils to grow more suitable flowers in neglected areas.

Lobby your council to let some roadside verges flower (where they are away from road junctions and it is safe to do so).

Allow lawns to flower.

Talk to local farmers that have meadows, asking them to stagger their hay meadow harvest timing to allow late flowers to bloom.

Encourage and support local farmers and landowners to seed their field margins with wild flowers.

Moss Carder Bee (*Bombus muscorum*)

There are four predominantly brown bumblebees known in the UK and two of them appear to be in steep decline, including the Moss carder bee. Once common and widespread in Britain this bee has declined severely and is now a UK BAP Priority species.

The Moss carder bee is a long-tongued bumblebee feeding on long tubular flowers such as dead nettles, clover, and yellow rattle. It's a pretty bee with a gingery back pack (thorax) and soft yellow-banded abdomen with creamy yellow sides. It is difficult to distinguish from the equally rare Brown-banded carder bee (*Bombus humilis*). And to the untrained eye it also resembles the Common carder bee of similar size and colouring (but without the ginger back pack). To make ID even more difficult some of the carder bees fade and lose their hairs in late summer and then even the bee experts can struggle to tell them all apart.

The queens of the Moss carder bee are the largest of the carder bees while the males and workers are of a similar, but smaller size.

The pretty Moss carder bee is so-called because it nests in mossy patches and gathers moss and dry grass to cover its nest. Like the Brown-banded carder bee it nests on maritime and coastal heath and grassland and needs flower rich heath and grassland to survive. If your garden borders this type of environment then you might be blessed with these bees in your garden, but it is a rare beauty and more likely to be spotted while out with a bee expert in suitable habitat.

Like most true bumblebees it is a social bee, which means it lives as a 'family unit' with a small colony of workers, just 40–120 (*Ref 22 and 23*) and it doesn't forage far from its nest, visiting long tubular flowers from the pea family such as vetch and

The pretty Moss carder bee (Bombus muscorum) is a rare ginger beauty. © BBCT/Nick Owens

clover, plants in the figwort family (scrophulariaceae) such as yellow rattle, and the mint family (lamiaceae) such as betony (*Stachys officinalis*).

Special behaviour/how to spot

It's not easy to spot this bee, partly because it's rare and also because it is similar to a few other species. Look online to see if there have been any sightings near you or team up with your local branch of the Bumblebee Conservation Trust and join their bee walks to learn how to identify these bees and find out more about them. Find out more about its usual nesting habitat and see if there are any areas in your neighbourhood that may support this species.

Cuckoo bee – this is another host species for the Field cuckoo bee (*Bombus campestris*).

How you can help

Grow more plants from the pea family such as vetches and clover etc.

Plant dead nettles such as *Lamium purpureum* and *Lamium maculatum* and *Lamium album* to flower in early spring. These are great early food plants for all the long tongued bumblebees.

The Field cuckoo bee (Bombus campestris) has several host species including the Moss carder bee (Bombus muscorum).
© BBCT/Shona Menzies

Allow moss to grow around your plot for nesting bees and try not to disturb any potential nesting sites.

Join the Bumblebee Conservation Trust and bee walk with an expert who can help you spot and identify bees in a garden setting. Take the children and join a bee treasure hunt where the prize is finding a rare species, it's like a real life game of Pokémon and could be just the way to get the kids inspired.

If you find a nest try to leave it alone and let the bees complete their lifecycle. Unless the nest is threatened, they are unlikely to sting and are a huge benefit to the plants in your garden.

HELP! I'VE GOT A BUMBLEBEE NEST

Bumblebees do nest in gardens and often under sheds, in compost bins or in bird boxes. The colonies don't usually last more than three or four months so think carefully about whether they are really doing any harm and see if you can live with them until their cycle is complete. Bumblebees rarely sting. They have an important role in pollinating plants and add to the rich biodiversity in your garden.

Remember the positive things about having a nest nearby; you can observe the development of the colony and your garden plants will be properly pollinated. A garden without bees is a dead garden. Bumblebees will only sting if they are threatened, and moving their nest is a full on threat, so if you can live without disturbing them and they aren't going to cause major problems, it's better to let them live out their life cycle and enjoy them. Put a sign up to protect the nest and let others know its location.

If that's really not possible get some advice from a local wildlife trust or group who may know someone that can assist. The Bumblebee Conservation Trust has a helpful FAQ page on its website. (*Ref 24*)

A bumblebee nest in the garden is a blessing. Warn other garden users with a sign and watch them come and go, but don't disturb. © *Jean Vernon*

SPECIALIST AND RARE SOLITARY BEES

Of the 276 species in the UK, around 250 of them are solitary bees, which don't usually live as part of a community and basically function alone. The female bees are the single mums of the bee world, mating with males of the same species but then abandoned to make their nest, lay their eggs and complete their lifecycle alone.

With over two hundred and fifty different species of solitary bees in the UK you won't find them all in this book. First because it's not a textbook, second because you may not see them in and around your garden. Many of them don't even look like bees. I'm going to concentrate on those you might find and those that have an interesting story to tell.

Just like the bumblebees, there are some solitary bees that need specific plants to complete their lifecycle. And when those plants are spread out or less common in our gardens or the wider environment, that's when these bees may struggle to survive and become in danger of extinction. It's a bit like only being able to do your shopping at a really specialist shop and having to carry your shopping home by hand. And the shop may only open at certain random times of the week. If you can't get there when it's open your store cupboards can become bare quite quickly, and even if you stock up when it is open you can only carry so much home. Our unpredictable weather dictates

Some bees, like the Long-horned bee, depend on just a few species of flowers for their survival. © *Liam Olds*

when bees can get out to collect their food. If the flowers are only available for feeding at certain times of the year, unless the weather is OK and the bees can get to the food source, they are at risk of starving. It's tough out there.

Fussy Eaters

Some bees have a lifecycle that totally and absolutely coincides with when their food plants are in flower. These are usually bees that are very specific in their feeding needs, visiting just a few plants within a plant genus. These bees are described as being oligolectic and rely on recognising their food plants by using visual and olfactory (smell) floral clues. (*Ref 25*)

Sometimes the choice of food plants depends on the length of the bee's tongue. Just like the bumblebees, short-tongued bees for example can't reach into the longer corollas of some flowers, although, bees being bees, sometimes they cheat (see nectar robbing). The problem with this is that the flowering time of the food plants needs to absolutely match the emergence of the bee species. Imagine having spent all winter hunkered down under your duvet only to find that all the supermarkets and restaurants are shut when you emerge in spring and that there's nothing in the cupboard either. You would simply starve, and they do too. That's why it's so very, very important for gardeners to grow a wide variety of plants with different flower shapes that are in flower in every season but especially in autumn, late winter and early spring.

Critical Timing

Other bees that are more generalist in their feeding habits (described scientifically as being polylectic) gather pollen and nectar from a variety of plants. Again these bees may be restricted to the types of flowers that they can feed on by the length of their tongues. This can vary within a species group, but long-tongued bees tend to feed on plants in the pea (legume) family such as bird's foot trefoil, the vetches as well as clovers, but also on other flowers such as the deadnettles (lamium) and those with a long corolla like comfrey and salvias.

So even though they are generalists they too can be affected by a lack of suitable food plants that coincide with their life cycle. Short-tongued bees will visit flowers that provide more accessible nectar, such as the dinner plate pads of the daisy family and the lacy platforms of the umbellifers (now correctly called Apiaceae). Flower shape is really important for different bee species, and a gardener wishing to plant for the bees really needs to choose plants suitable for long and short tongued species, avoiding the overbred, double blousy blooms that may have sacrificed nectaries for extra petals. Remember too that little bees can balance and feed on tiny flowers, but big bees need sturdy stems to support their weight.

FLOWER SHAPES

A few examples of flower shapes.

Open single flowers such as species and wild roses. Here the stamens are accessible offering a pollen source to the bees.

This Orange-tailed mining bee (Andrena haemorrhoa) can climb into this open rose flower and collect the accessible pollen.
© Jean Vernon

Bowl shaped flowers where the petals protect the pollen and nectar, such as crocus, hellebores and poppies.

The petals of this poppy form a bowl that provides protection for the pollinators. The flower entices them inside with copious protein rich pollen. © Jean Vernon

Dinner plate flowers where the central flower boss contains dozens or hundreds of tiny flowers in one place such as coneflowers, sun flowers, daisies etc.

A large flat open flower presents a safe landing platform for insects offering a 'dinner plate' of individual flowers to plunder for nectar. © Martin Mulchinock

Umbellifers (now called *Apiaceae*) offer a lacy landing site for lightweight pollinators to land and feed, such as wild carrot, white lace flower (*Orlaya grandiflora*) fennel, lovage and the sea hollies (eryngiums).

The tiny flowers, held en masse on lacy heads of the wild carrot are just some of the amazing plants in the Apiaceae family, beloved by pollinators. © Jean Vernon

Tubular flowers where the nectar is contained deep inside the flower, such as foxgloves, penstemons, salvias, comfrey and clovers.

Flowers with tubular corollas like salvia need a long-tongued bee to reach into the flower and effect pollination. © Martin Mulchinock

Pea shaped flowers, such as vetches, sweetpeas, peas and beans, where the bee has to learn how to force open the flower to access the pollen and nectar, requiring a stronger bee for pollination.

Pea flowers like this perennial sweetpea need careful navigation for the bee to reach the nectar prize. © Jean Vernon

INTRODUCING THE SOLITARY BEES

These are the bees that don't live in a social group like bumblebees and honeybees; instead there are just males and females.

The males pretty much always emerge out of the nest first after winter has passed, usually about two weeks before the females. That's quite interesting in itself. They will feed themselves on available flowers, supping nectar from suitable early flowering plants and they will wait eagerly for the females to emerge. They can be so keen that they have been known to literally drag the females out of the nest before they emerge. But mostly they just hang around the nest, waiting for the 'girls'. This system ensures that the females are well mated: imagine if the females hatched first and there were no male bees around? They could be eaten before they could mate and lay their eggs.

Once mated she makes a nest or prepares a burrow and lays the eggs of the females at the back of the nest and the males in the front. How she knows to do this is unclear, but what it does mean is that if the nest is attacked by a predator, maybe a woodpecker, then it is the developing male bees that are devoured first, and the precious females (who will ensure the survival of the species) might just survive deeper in the nest.

The males emerging first is also thought to improve the genetic diversity of the bee colonies, because the males should disperse a bit by moving around to other nests nearby and hopefully mate with females from another family line and not with their own sisters.

The females work very, very hard and do it all by themselves, hence the single mum label I have given them. They have to forage and feed themselves, choose a suitable partner and mate quickly before they make a nest and lay their eggs. The nest itself can be a work of art and is almost always an effort, except perhaps for the cavity-nesting bees that make use of existing nooks and crannies, hollow stems and woodworm holes.

But even these cavities are prepared and often lined with incredible attention to detail, using sometimes extraordinary materials from in and around your garden.

Every egg that is laid is carefully positioned in a prepared cell that has been provisioned with food for the larva as it develops and hatches. So the single female solitary bee has a lot to do. She has to collect pollen, wet it with nectar and make a food ball for each egg that she lays. She has to find, make or excavate a nest, prepare the nest cells and lay an egg in each and she may make several nests before she dies, leaving her offspring to hatch, feed, make a cocoon, pupate and overwinter until they emerge as adult solitary bees next spring. She will never meet her young.

With over 250 species of solitary bees in the UK, there's not room in this book to include them all, and anyway it's far too complicated. Add to that the fact that some are so small (like an ant) or so rare, or aren't really garden bees at all, that you'd need an expert bee guide to describe them all. Fortunately, recently (2015) naturalist and bee aficionado Steven Falk published the perfect book: *Field Guide to the Bees of Great Britain and Ireland.* So if this book has whetted your appetite for more bee knowledge, Stephen's book is a must read. (See Further Reading for more bee reading material).

THE SECRET LIVES OF GARDEN BEES

The simplest way to understand and learn more about solitary bees is to divide them into ground nesting bees and aerial nesting bees and then describe some of the most common, interesting and specialist bees within each section. But remember that there are always exceptions.

GROUND NESTING BEES

These bees nest in the soil. Around 68 species of the aptly named mining bees are in the genus Andrena, *(Ref 26)* some of which are the earliest emerging solitary bees and many are common in and around our gardens and in public parks and open spaces. The females collect pollen on their hind legs and nest in sandy soil where they excavate burrows around the base of garden shrubs, on short mown grass or in sandy banks.

Some of them have fantastic common names, like the rare Carrot mining bee (*Andrena nitidiuscula*), *(Ref 27 and 28)* which feeds on the flowers of wild carrot and wild parsnip. There's a Chocolate mining bee (*Andrena scotica*), which looks a bit like a honeybee and is often seen foraging in spring gardens. And there are Mini mining bees, such as *Andrena minutula*, which as the name suggests are miniature-mining bees, fairly common and also ground nesting. The Pantaloon bee (*Dasypoda hirtipes*), as its name suggests has very long, pollen collecting hairs on its rear legs, giving it the effect of large gingery velvet trousers or pantaloons.

Just like its name suggests, the Pantaloon bee (Dasypoda hirtipes) looks like it's wearing fabulous trousers.
© Shutterstock/Henrik Larsson

The pretty markings of the Andrena cineraria gives it a panda-like persona. © Liam Olds

Ashy Mining Bee (*Andrena cineraria*)

The Ashy mining bee is one of the earliest mining bees that you might find in your garden. It's quite distinctive, sometimes affectionately called the panda bee, because of its markings; it is mostly black with patches of soft grey/white hairs. The females have a shiny black abdomen with two bands of light grey hair across the thorax and a furry white face. The adults emerge in spring, from March onwards, and these bees are on the wing until mid summer.

How to spot

The Ashy mining bee is pretty easy to spot because it looks very distinctive.

You might spot them foraging on early flowering blackthorn, hawthorn and fruit blossom. But it is the nests of these little mining bees that are the giveaway sign that they are in and around your garden. Look carefully at the closely mown, bare patches on your lawn, especially if you have sandy soil. The entrance to the nest of an Ashy mining bee looks like a little volcano, with piles of sandy soil domed up into a little cone with a hole in the top where the female comes and goes.

If you've got mini volcano-like piles of soil in your garden you may have the Ashy mining bee nesting there. © Jean Vernon

Look out for the bee flies in spring. This one, the dotted bee fly (Bombylius discolor), flicks its eggs into the nests of the Ashy mining bee. © Brigit Strawbridge Howard

Even though these bees are solitary, they do nest in numbers close together, so you might find one little volcano or a cluster of several. This is known as nesting in aggregation and although the nests are numerous and close together these bees are not part of a larger community, they are simply taking advantage of the ideal nesting conditions of the area. The female will close the hole in bad weather and when she has ceased foraging for the day.

Another sign that you might have the Ashy mining bee nearby is the presence of the Dotted bee fly (*Bombylius discolor*), which is a parasite of the Ashy mining bee.

How to help
Leave the dandelions to flower as they are essential sources of pollen and nectar for these bees.

Replace a garden boundary with a flowering hedge including blackthorn, hawthorn, wild cherry, willow and plums.

Leave a patch of lawn with bare soil, or an area of the flower border undisturbed.

Plant fruit trees around the garden, including a crab apple as a general pollinator plant for other apples in your locality.

OTHER MINING BEES TO LOOK OUT FOR

The Tawny mining bee (*Andrena fulva*) is another common mining bee that emerges in spring. She has bright red thorax and abdomen, and nests, like the Ashy mining bee, in lawns or short mown grass banks, leaving the tell-tale volcano spoil heaps where the nests are excavated.

The Chocolate mining bee (*Andrena scotica*) looks quite similar to a honeybee to the untrained eye, but this is a common mining bee you may see in and around your garden. It is known to nest in odd places around buildings and you may find it in your spring garden.

One of the first mining bees I found it my garden was the Early mining bee, or the Orange-tailed mining bee (*Andrena haemorrhoa*). It's a bit slimmer and smaller than a honeybee and has a fluffy, orange red thorax and a slinky black abdomen. It's a pretty common solitary bee in gardens and a good one to look out for.

The Yellow-legged mining bee (*Andrena flavipes*) (*Ref 29*) might look to the amateur like a honeybee; it's a similar size and has banding on its abdomen. It has orange pollen brushes on its rear legs. This bee is fairly common in southern Britain and Wales and thought to be spreading northwards. It can have two generations in one year, peaking in spring and mid summer, when you may see them.

Look out for the pretty Tawny mining bee (Andrena fulva) in your spring garden. © Liam Olds

Identifying the solitary bees is not easy. Andrena flavipes *has a stripy abdomen so it resembles a honeybee.*
© Jean Vernon

The Grey patch mining bee (*Andrena nitida*) is another common mining bee in the southern UK counties. It has a bright gingery red thorax that looks like a backpack and a black shiny abdomen bearing tufts of grey hairs at the sides.

The Mini-mining bee (*Andrena minutula*) is another common garden bee, though it can be difficult to identify from the other closely related species. Look out for very small bees feeding on garden plants and you may have this little beauty nesting nearby.

*Look out for the grey tufted abdomen that indicates that the Grey patch mining bee (*Andrena nitida*) is in your garden.* © Brigit Strawbridge Howard

OTHER SPECIES OF MINING BEES

The furrow bees include the Lasioglossum and Halictus bees, (*Ref 30*) which include around 40 species. These are mostly soil nesting bees that collect pollen underneath their abdomens and on their legs. They are difficult to tell apart so unless you are experienced you will need some expert advice for identification.

There's an amazing, small, metallic green Lasioglossum bee (*Lasioglossum morio*), which is widespread and fairly common in flower rich habitats in the UK.

The pretty Furrow bees are generally small and can share their nest entrance, giving the impression of a social community. © Liam Olds

Long-Horned Bee (*Eucera longicornis*)

Some bees are easier to identify just because of their appearance, and this one, the Long-horned bee (*Ref 31 and Ref 32*) is one of those. As its name suggests it has extremely long antennae, much longer than that of any other bee, which gives it a really endearing look. Like most bees it is the males that have the longest antennae but for the Long-horned bee it's been taken to the extreme, with its antennae longer than its body. How it flies without crashing is a mystery. Sadly it's another rare bee, largely occurring in southern Britain and specifically around the Devon coastline and in Wales where it nests on the coast.

These bees nest *en-masse* in the soft rock cliffs, and are often so clustered together that it might seem like they are a social nester. It's the presence of just the right conditions for nesting that attracts many females to nest together, and when the males first emerge in spring they are less than subtle, staking out the nest sites and suitable food plants, waiting for the females to emerge. These bees are on the wing from May to July, with the males more prevalent earlier in the season in May and June and the females nest building after mating. They feed predominantly on flowers of the pea family so plants like the bird's foot trefoil (*Lotus corniculatus*) are an excellent source of nectar, as are kidney vetch (*Anthyllis vulneria*), red clover (*Trifolium pratense*), white clover (*Trifolium repens*), and many of the vetches and peas. They have a particular liking for meadow vetchling (*Lathyrus pratensis*).

The unmistakable huge antennae of the male Long-horned bee. © Liam Olds

How to spot

You can't fail to recognize the over-endowed males, which wave their huge antennae like oversized eyebrows in that kind of cartoony way that only a bee can do.

Look out for the males buzzing about soft rock cliff faces on the south coast. They have one thing on their mind and they are unlikely to be bothered by you. Find a local food source for they will also stake out the food plants too in the hope of intercepting a foraging female. A good bet is the meadow vetchling (*Lathyrus pratensis*), with its bright yellow, pea-like flowers.

Though rare, you might just be lucky enough to find these in your garden if you live in southern Britain and particularly around the south Devon and Welsh coast. Think of them as lost treasure and see what else you can find while you look for them.

Otherwise, if you are really keen you could sign up for a bee identification course or book a holiday cottage in June in an area where they are known and try to find them. It's a great quest to get the kids involved with, especially if they have a leaning towards nature. The little ones will love the dalekesque antennae of these bees, and who knows what else you might find.

How to help

Allow clovers and vetches and perennial sweet peas to grow in your garden; these will feed all sorts of bees and be good to support your garden's biodiversity.

Learn more about this rare species by reading more about it. Visit coastal sites with a bee expert and see if you can spot this bee.

Report any sightings to BWARS with a location, an image and as much information as you can gather; this bee is in decline and it is important for the experts to understand its distribution.

Ivy Bee (*Colletes hederae*)

As the name suggests this bee forages almost exclusively on ivy. It's a fairly recent addition to the UK's bee fauna and our only true autumnal bee; it's the last bee species to emerge in the UK. The Ivy bee is a solitary bee that was first recorded in the UK in 2001 having arrived from Europe. The freshly emerging bees appear in September just as the wild ivy (*Hedera helix*) is in flower, providing the Ivy bees and many other pollinators with essential pollen and nectar at this late point of the season.

These are ground nesting bees that build their nests in suitable soil; the eggs mature and pupate underground before the adults start emerging in September. They may be seen *en masse* flying fast over the soil, seemingly together in social behaviour, but while they can be present in large numbers these are actually individual bees going about their business, seeking food and mating partners in the short time that the ivy is in flower. These bees are quite strikingly stripy with very distinct yellow and dark brown stripes on their bodies.

Take a closer look at the ivy flowers to see a strikingly stripy bee that is associated with this plant: the Ivy bee.
© Liam Olds

Special behaviour/how to spot

This is a very stripy bee, with distinct yellow and dark brown markings. Seen around large stands of flowering ivy on sunny days, these solitary bees generally only fly in bright, dry weather. You can spot it feeding on wild ivy in autumn, but also emerging from ground nesting holes in early September. You may see many of these bees flying low over the ground rather frantically in early September. To the untrained eye it looks a bit like a wasp.

How you can help

Let ivy grow and flower in your garden. Gardeners can make a huge difference to these bees by allowing the wild ivy to flower. It supports other wildlife too; ivy clad outbuildings provide roosting and nesting sites for birds, especially sparrows.

Avoid digging over areas of soil where you know these bees to be nesting. And always leave an area of soil undisturbed in any garden to ensure any mining bees can develop underground.

You can report sightings of the Ivy bee as part of a BWARS (Bees, Wasps & Ants Recording Society) citizen science project (*Ref 33*) that is plotting the spread of this bee in the UK.

Yellow Loosestrife Bee (*Macropis europaea*)

This is a fairly rare solitary bee that may occur in your gardens if you have a bog garden area or are near a river, and its food plant yellow loosestrife (*Lysimachia vulgaris*) is growing in or near your garden. The Yellow loosestrife bee (*Ref 34 and Ref 35*) is a very specialist bee for several reasons.

First it is what the experts call monolectic, feeding pretty much exclusively on yellow loosestrife of which, of course it then becomes its main pollinator. It's a very fragile relationship; if one partner is not present then the other will die out. And while the Yellow loosestrife bee has been recorded feeding on nectar from a few other plants, such as bird's foot trefoil (*Lotus corniculatus*) and bramble (*Rubus fruticosus*), that may be because the yellow loosestrife does not have nectaries and these bees do need to find a source of energy-rich food to sustain their activities.

Instead the bright yellow flowers secrete a floral oil that the bees gather and mix with pollen that they then lay their eggs on. Like many solitary bees they make their nests in banks or flat ground. The nest is shallow and marked by the presence of a sandy volcano-like mound, and inside, a long shallow burrow leads to slightly angled 'dead end' cells where the female places the pollen and oil loaf and lays her eggs. But what is unique about this bee is that she lines her nest with the floral oil of the yellow loosestrife, perhaps to waterproof it and protect her developing young.

If you find a bee on the yellow loosestrife there's a good chance it is the Yellow loosestrife bee. Look closely for its unique yoga-like stance. © Brigit Strawbridge Howard

How to spot this bee

The Yellow loosestrife bee is mostly found in southern England from Devon across to Kent and into Somerset and Norfolk, and unless you have a stand of yellow loosestrife and a boggy area then you are unlikely to see it. When it does occur it can be in larger numbers. The best way to spot it is to stake out any established clumps of yellow loosestrife over the summer months, July to August and into September. The males have a distinctive yellow face and are quite territorial and will patrol the plants when they are in flower looking for a mate. But the females have another interesting and unusual tactic that they are thought to use as a defence against the males. They have a defensive posture described by Waldemar Celary (*Ref 36*) as kicking females, with their hind legs extended above their abdomen to reject the pouncing males. If you spend time looking for this bee, you may be rewarded with the sight of little sticky-up legs poking out the yellow flowers, and then you will know for sure you have found the female Yellow loosestrife bee.

How to help

You can guess the best way to assist this bee: you need to grow more yellow loosestrife and if possible create a boggy area or marginal wet garden beside a pond on your plot. This unusual bee also needs other sources of nectar to support its lifecycle so grow some nectar rich plants such as the knapweeds and the lacy landing pads of the nectar rich umbellifers.

AERIAL AND CAVITY NESTING BEES

These are the bees that nest in our bee houses, woodworm holes, hollow plant stems and other nooks and crannies. They come in all shapes and sizes; from the tiniest bee, like the Campanula bee to the common or garden mason bees (Osmia species). With a bee house you can observe some of these bees making a nest then lining the cells with a variety of garden materials, including leaves, mud and plant fibres.

The Wool Carder Bee (*Anthidium manicatum*)

Oh how I love this bee, possibly because one of the garden plants it is often associated with, lamb's ear (*Stachys byzantina*), was one of my favourite childhood plants. We always had a big patch in the garden and I just loved picking the soft furry grey leaves and brushing them against my face. I can't say I ever noticed the bee activity that may have been going on there, but it's a plant close to my heart and I still grow it today. But back to the bee.

The Wool carder bee gets its name from its nest-building activities. The females shave the woolly hairs off plant stems and leaves to line their nest cells, and lamb's ears is one of the plants it does this to. Its perfect bunny ear shaped leaves are just

Find a clump of lamb's ears in summer and sit and wait to see if there are Wool carder bees in your garden. © Jean Vernon

covered in soft grey fur; well it's not fur of course, it is dense leaf hairs that the plant uses to protect its leaves from intense sunshine and reduce evaporation at the leaf surface. But the whorls of its soft pink flowers are also a good source of nectar and it is around established clumps of this plant where you can often find these bees in summer. The Wool carder bee is widespread in the UK but its distribution in more northern regions is less clear. (*Ref 37*)

The Wool carder bee is a common garden bee; it is quite dark in appearance with yellow spots down the sides of the abdomen and yellow markings on the face and on the legs.

The males are larger than the females and are very territorial. They will stake out a prime feeding spot waiting for a female and defend their patch from other males and other large insects, including bumblebees and hoverflies. The males will chase off other bees of other species in their quest to find their mate. The males have spiky spines at the tip of their abdomen and brandish them like weapons when defending their territory. Like many other solitary bees the males emerge from the nests first, usually around June when their food plants are in flower. The females emerge a couple of weeks later and by this time the males are ready and waiting. The female bees collect pollen to provision the eggs on their underside, collecting the grains between the rear facing hairs underneath (*Ref 38*). As with the Leaf-cutter bee, this makes them excellent pollinators as they move pollen from flower to flower.

How to spot
These bees are on the wing in the summer months, usually between June and August. If you are lucky you might see them nesting in a bee house.

Look out for the female bees taking the fluff from hairy plants such as lamb's ears and other stachys species.

On a warm summers day spend some time watching a clump of lamb's ears for this bee's unique behaviour. Look out for the aggressive territorial behaviour by the male Wool carder bee.

They have distinctive yellow markings down the sides of their abdomen and the male has pointy spines at the base of his abdomen.

These are aerial nesters and will nest in an artificial bee house providing the hollow tubes suit their needs, but in the wild they will choose old beetle holes in dead wood and hollow stems. The female uses the soft plant hairs that she collects to line the nest cells where she also positions a ball of pollen for the developing larvae to eat.

How to help
Grow the food plants that this species needs-mints, toadflax, vetches and legumes as well as clumps of lamb's ear.

Provide nesting sites by installing a quality bee nesting house. But manage them. Don't just set them up and then leave them to their own devices. They do need cleaning and care at the end of the season.

Leave stacks of rotten wood for the insects to nest and overwinter.

Watch the live clip of these bees on the BWARS website; it will help you to identify them in your garden.

Spend time looking for this summer bee and if you find it, make a report to BWARS.

The Mason Bees *(Osmia species)*

There are several species of mason bees and these are some of the most common solitary bees you may find in your garden. If you install a bee house or bee nesting block it is most likely to be used by mason bees. There are eleven species in the UK and the most well known is the Red mason bee (*Osmia bicornis*) which is common in England and Wales but scarce in Scotland and Ireland.

It's a really efficient pollinator of fruit trees and can be introduced to orchards to improve pollination. In a garden setting with one or two apple trees that need pollinating, a mason bee nest would offer a fantastic pollination solution and a better option than a honeybee hive. The Red mason bee is the only solitary bee that is available to buy commercially. Some claims suggest that one single mason bee can do the pollination work of 120 honeybees, which makes them an excellent bee to encourage in your garden if you have fruit trees. These bees are safe for children because they don't sting. Mason bees collect mud to seal their nest cells.

If you want a better harvest from your fruit trees, do what you can to attract mason bees to your plot. The Red mason bee is an excellent pollinator. © Brigit Strawbridge Howard

How to spot

The Red mason bee is pretty easy to spot feeding on fruit trees in spring, or nesting in old brickwork or collecting mud. They are a common nester in garden bee boxes, but will also nest in hollow stems, window frames and other aerial cavities. The females have an orange red furry abdomen and black heads with inward curving antennae, which is unusual in solitary bees. These bees collect pollen underneath their abdomen on a brush.

How to help

Leave a mud patch in the garden and keep it wet so that these bees have material to seal their nests.

Grow more fruit trees, especially crab apples, apples and pears, to feed the bees and provide a fruit harvest for your family.

Plant plenty of spring flowers that will blossom when these bees emerge in April.

You can buy special cardboard tubes that the mason bees like to nest in, or invest in a quality bee house to provide good nesting places for these bees.

Get the children involved in watching and looking after these bees so that they associate bees with the flowers, the environment and even the food on the table. Make your own bee Pokémonesque game using bee identification cards, giving them points for every bee they spot and identify.

The Snail Nester Bee (*Osmia bicolor*)

There are also some very specialist members of the mason bee genus (Osmia) including the Snail nester bee, also called the Red-tailed mason bee (*Osmia bicolor*).

It's pretty unlikely you'll find this bee in your garden, but I just have to share it with you so that you can see the amazing ingenuity and diversity of our wonderful bees. There are three species of bee that use snail shells to make a nest. Instead of using hollow stems and cavities or burrowing into the soil to make suitable cavities to lay their eggs, these bees are nature's recyclers, like little hermit bees, making use of old, discarded snail shells. One of these bees, also called the Thatcher bee (*Osmia bicolor*) is even more ingenious. It was featured on *The One Show* in 2015 with naturalist John Waters and if you search you can find the clip online. (*Ref 39*) The female bee not only collects pollen for her larvae to eat as they grow and pupate into adults, but she also positions the snail shell in such a way so that rain doesn't fall into the opening and then she weighs down the shell with little bits of stone to keep it in place. Once she is satisfied that her eggs are safe and provided for, she then seals up the snail shell with a leaf mastic, a trick that has gained her the name of 'pesto bee' by bee enthusiast Brigit Strawbridge Howard. But the Snail nester bee hasn't finished even now. For the next three hours or so this little bee goes off and picks up blades of grass and then like a witch on a broomstick she carries each piece of grass back to her snail shell nest and literally thatches around the shell until it is camouflaged in the undergrowth.

Some bees nest in empty snail shells. These waterproof dens offer perfect protection for developing bees. © *Richard Comont*

And if that's not enough, this one, single mother bee will repeat the process with up to 20 empty snail shells over the course of about two months, often laying just one egg or two in each, until she runs out of energy and dies. The camouflaged snail shell will protect the developing new bees through the rest of the season, over the winter and up until the adult bees emerge in early spring. The male bees hatch first in February and are ready and waiting for the females to emerge in March.

How to spot

The Snail nester bees are downland bees, so you are pretty unlikely to see them in your garden; nevertheless it's possible, depending on where you live. Look for snail shells sealed with green masticated leaves, think pesto and you get the idea. But look, don't disturb. The new adult bees will emerge in March and April and then the process of procuring snail shells begins. If you think you might have this bee nearby then set some snail shells out in a known spot in February or March and mark them, then return to check on them from time to time.

In nest building season, April and May, there is only one bee that will fly around with pieces of long grass. It really does look like the broomstick-riding witch, or a unicorn bee, so it's a great way to spot them. You might also notice bees flying with small stones, these are the weights that she will use to stabilise the shells. Watch where she flies to and observe her nest building. She's a beautiful dark bee with a rusty orange striped abdomen, but you are unlikely to see the nest as it is so well camouflaged.

How to help

By just being aware that anywhere in the countryside or your garden could be a nesting site for bees and by treating nature with the care and respect it deserves, you will help. These bees, like many others, have special needs and special behaviours. Leaving snail shells in clusters around your garden for all wildlife is a good place to start. Share the story of the snail-nesting bee with others, especially children. Search out the videos online and watch them with the awe and wonder they deserve and then look out for these amazing creatures as you bathe in nature and all its wonders.

Scissor Bees *(Chelostoma species)*

The scissor bees (*Ref 40*) include two British bee species; both are totally dependent on one plant group (i.e. a small number of species), giving them the technical description of being oligolectic. One feeds on buttercups and nests in dead wood, hollow stems and thatched roofs and sleeps in flowers giving it its idiosyncratic name of *Chelostoma florisomne*, far more descriptive than its common name, Large scissor bee, because florisomne means flower sleeper.

The Large scissor bee feeds on buttercups and is known to sleep inside the flowers. © *Steven Falk*

The other is the Campanula bee or the Harebell carpenter bee (*Chelostoma campanularum*) (*Ref 41, 42 & 43*)

The Small campanula bee (also called the Small scissor bee) is truly the smallest UK bee, measuring just a few millimetres (5-6mm) in length. There are actually two species of solitary bees that specialise in feeding on the pollen of campanulas – the second is also called a Campanula bee but looks very different and is larger.

The Small campanula bee doesn't really look like what most people think a bee should look like, it looks more like a long-bodied black fly. Also as it's so small it is often overlooked as being a bee, even though it can be a frequent visitor to many gardens. This small, slender black bee can be found in gardens from midsummer

Take a closer look at the campanula flowers in your garden. The UK's smallest bee, Chelostoma campanularum feeds only on campanulas. © Steven Falk

until the middle of August, predominantly in southern England. It's so tiny in fact that unless you are looking for it, you might not even see it, but clusters of male campanula bees will congregate around open campanula flowers in summer and can actually overnight together inside campanula flowers, and can be found, sometimes for days, huddled together in flowers, especially in dull, damp weather. Cute as this may sound, since these bees usually mate inside the flowers, it is likely that should a female arrive to collect pollen, she will have the undivided attention of several males and mate successfully in the pretty blue bell shaped flowers. The male has two prongs at the base of its abdomen, (*Ref 44*) which you can see using a hand lens. The females have white hairs underneath to collect the pollen.

But this little bee needs a special group of plants to survive. It feeds on the pollen and nectar from harebells (campanulas), on mostly what are called the nettle leaved (*Campanula trachelium*) and clustered bellflower (*Campanula glomerata*), both of these are popular garden plants. Some campanulas grow wild (especially the true harebell *Campanula rotundifolia*).

They are also known to feed on the nectar of some garden geraniums (cranesbill). It's the female that collects the pollen by landing inside the flowers on the pollen-laden anthers, which she grips between her mandibles and her front legs. Her back legs push the dusty white pollen back so that the grains are stored in the pollen collecting hairs under her abdomen. They are also known to rub their abdomen against the pollen-laden anthers. She will use this pollen to provide food for her eggs that she lays in tiny woodworm holes and dry, thin hollow stems. The males simply feed on nectar, mostly from campanulas but also from hardy geraniums (cranesbill).

Special behaviour/how to spot
Stake out your garden harebells and bellflowers in early summer. Look for clusters of little black insects, around 6mm long. Males hang out in the bell shaped flowers at night and in damp weather. It's more common in southern Britain so if you garden further north don't despair if you can't find it, and visit other gardens such as Kew Gardens where it is known.

Use a magnifying glass or hand lens to look at the bees. The males have a pronounced fork at the base of their abdomen.

How you can help
Grow a range of campanulas in your garden. These are pretty garden plants, ideal for a cottage style garden, but there are also several varieties suitable for rock gardens, pots and the front of the border. Good ones to grow are the cluster bellflowers, which have clusters of flowers on each flower stem (*Campanula glomerata*) and the nettle leaved bellflowers (*Campanula trachelium*), which unsurprisingly, have leaves that resemble nettles.

But studies suggest that the popular milky bellflower (*Campanula lactiflora*) with its milky white (or blue) flowers is not such a good forage plant for these bees. Scientists have discovered that the flowers lack specific volatiles (scent) that the bees may use to distinguish and find the plants with the exact pollen that they seek. The research concludes that while colour (of the flowers) is important for flower recognition by the bees, it is the presence of these floral scent bouquets that are key for the bees to recognise the plants with the pollen that they need. (*Ref 45*)

The small campanula bee uses woodworm holes as a hollow tube to create individual provisioned (with pollen and nectar) egg chambers where they lay their eggs. So if you have a rotting tree stump riddled with beetle holes or even a shed or fence with woodworm, leave it *in situ*, as these tiny holes are the perfect place for these bees to lay their eggs. A bundle of dry reeds, chive stems and grasses, trimmed with their hollow ends revealed and placed in a sheltered dry place may provide an alternative place for these bees to nest.

This bee is a type of mason bee and requires mud to seal its egg chambers, so a bog garden or available muddy/puddled area with wet soil provides the essential mud needed to assist its nesting activity. A source of mud near to nests means the bees expend less vital energy searching and gathering this material.

The Leaf-Cutter Bees (*Megachile* species)

The Leaf-cutter bee is one group of solitary bee species that most gardeners are familiar with, mostly because these bees leave tell-tale signs all around the garden that they are alive and active. Actually there are eight UK species of Leaf-cutter bees *(Ref 46)* and once you get to recognise these cute little bees you will see more and more of them around your garden. These solitary bees rarely sting and go about their business in your garden with little regard for human activity. They are simply fascinating to observe.

Leaf-cutter bees are so named because they cut out circular and semi circular sections out of garden leaves, most commonly roses, but leaves of other smooth leaved trees and shrubs can also be used, such as sycamore, wisteria and lilac.

She (it's always the females that do the work and nest building) stands on the leaf and cuts around her body and then flies off with the leaf segment to seal her egg chambers. Leaf-cutter bees do not eat the leaves of your plants and they are not garden pests. Plants that have had the Leaf-cutter bee treatment are not harmed or injured in any way and there is no need to worry about them. Never, ever try and control them or treat them as a pest, they are an absolute joy and are much better pollinators for your garden than honeybees. Plants affected will simply grow more leaves in due course. In fact it is a real pleasure to see the notches around the garden because it means these exceptional creatures are alive and well. The Leaf-cutter bees are excellent pollinators. This is because they are messy little bees and manage to get

This Leaf-cutter bee has taken advantage of some deep screw holes in a timber post. She has filled the hole top left and is now sealing the bottom hole. © Jean Vernon
Inset: The tell-tale signs of a leaf-cutter bee in your garden. © Jean Vernon

completely covered in pollen as they forage for food. They have a hairy underbelly designed to trap the pollen and as they move from flower to flower they transport the pollen grains to the female flower parts and pollination occurs.

Leaf-cutter bees prefer to nest in existing cavities, which makes them another of the bee species that are likely to nest in a bee box or insect house. They will also nest in the ground and some will even nest in neglected plant pots and abandoned hose reels (*Ref 47*). Each nest will contain about six individual cells and every one is supplied with a mix of pollen and nectar to feed the larva when it hatches out. The female eggs are positioned at the back of the nest and the males, which emerge first, are positioned at the front.

The Leaf-cutter bee actually lines the cavity with pieces of leaf and seals each cell with a leafy cap. Uncovered or excavated they look like mini cigars.

Some of these bees don't fly very far from their nest and so they are likely to make use of plants nearby and feed on flowers in close proximity. Leaf-cutter bees are also known to use flower petals instead of leaves.

Special behaviour/how to spot

Look out for little notches cut out of the leaves of garden shrubs but especially roses and azaleas. These are the signs that the Leaf-cutter bees are nesting nearby.

Keep an eye on pollen rich garden flowers, which these bees will visit to gather pollen to provision each egg that they lay. They are fascinating to watch and quite messy in their activity and are usually well dusted with pollen.

If you have a bee house or insect hotel it is often Leaf-cutter bees that populate the nesting tubes. Watch out for activity around May or June when the females may start to nest. They seal each egg chamber and the face of the nesting tube with a piece of leaf so they are quite easy to spot. They will also nest in natural cavities, hollow stems and other watertight narrow tubes, including old screw holes.

These bees are about the size of a honeybee with a slightly flatter

The female Leaf-cutter bee climbs right inside the cavity and lays the first female egg into a leaf lined cell at the back. She then pops out for more leaves and gradually fills the chamber.
© *Martin Mulchinock*

abdomen that is usually covered in pollen. They fly between May and September, feeding on garden flowers to sustain their activity.

How you can help
Plant more pollen rich flowers that are in flower in mid to late summer.

Grow more roses and shrubs to provide more nesting material.

Completely stop using pesticides in your garden. If you can only cut back on your spraying then avoid any chemical controls on flowering plants and especially on roses and plants with pollen rich flowers.

Grow more open, single, pollen rich flowers in your garden.

Place a bee house in the garden, or buy specialist nesting tubes for bees from a wildlife supplier and manage it properly.

INSECT HOUSES

You can create additional habitats for bees in your garden by making or buying a special insect house designed for aerial nesting solitary bees. When designed for bees and not as a piece of garden sculpture, these can and do attract a range of garden bees looking for suitable nesting sites, such as mason bees and Leaf-cutter bees. There are dozens of different designs and you can of course make your own. And the bees may even nest in some unlikely places in the garden. I once had a Leaf-cutter bee make a nest within the screw hole on a garden hose reel casing.

When it comes to insect houses, it's important to understand that the bees will spend many months inside these boxes, starting off as fertilised eggs and maturing into larvae and finally adults, so they are more than a temporary home for bees.

Unmanaged bee boxes and insect hotels can provide nesting sites for all manner of other garden creatures and mini beasts. In a large garden designed for wildlife, that may be perfectly OK, but if your intent is to have a bee box for the bees then you need to do a bit more than just give it space in your garden.

Whatever you do follow a few rules.

It's essential that the bees and larvae inside these insect houses, bee or insect boxes do not get wet or damp. They can usually withstand the cold but not the wet. Choose a design that is waterproof and be ready to move your chosen bee nest box into a cold but protected shed for the worst of the winter.

The bee box needs to face south for the very best results, that way it gets the best of the season's sun. But make sure it gets some shade during the day.

Look at the hollow tube diameter. Most of these bees use small diameter holes; woodworm hole size for the smallest bees, like the Campanula bee, up to 10mm maximum. Hollow tubes must have a closed end at the back; open-ended tubes are not suitable. Choose smooth tubes devoid of splinters and rough edges.

It's better to have separate houses offering one type of nesting tube rather than a huge diversity in one box.

Natural materials are the best; don't use plastic, which will create condensation and encourage mould and fungal problems that will affect the residents.

Choose a bee box that can be opened up for cleaning.

Protect the face of your bee box with chicken wire to prevent predators feasting on the developing bees.

Don't neglect your bee nest box from year to year. It needs to be managed to ensure that the bees survive and thrive. Most bee house designs will attract a few species of garden bees to nest, but it's important to understand that with these bees also come the predators and parasites that prey upon them. This is where it gets a bit scary because it's a bit like a version of *Alien* (*Ref 76*). But it's also important to note that everything has a place in nature, the food chain and in a healthy rich garden biodiversity, even what we perceive to be the baddies.

Solitary bee cells can become infested with pollen mites that hitch a ride on the adult bees and breed inside the protected climes inside a bee box. Over the course of time, remember it takes several months for the bee egg to mature to an adult, the cell can be completely overrun with pollen mites or other parasitic insects that may affect the development of the bee, or may even devour the egg before it becomes a larva. Then there's the cleptoparasite *Cacoxenus indagator*. It looks a bit like a fruit fly and can be seen hanging around bee boxes looking for pollen stores inside solitary bee egg cells. The adults will sneak in and if they find pollen they will lay their eggs in there. The unaware solitary bee will lay her own egg inside the chamber and the fly larvae will eat the pollen, causing the bee larva to starve to death, or they will eat the bee larva too. Once an insect house has been affected by these parasites, they can and do persist from season to season.

Not to mention the parasitoid wasps that seeks out the bee species that are their preferred host and enter the nest site to complete their lifecycle.

A badly managed bee box that attracts nesting solitary bees can be an unintentional magnet for some of these bee pests and inadvertently provide the parasites and mites with the perfect breeding ground.

While the presence of these bee 'pests' is an indication of a healthy population of the bees upon which they depend, let's be honest, most people that put a bee box in place are doing that to help the bees. If that's your intention but you don't want to manage or maintain your bee box then save your money and buy a bird box or a bat box instead and let the bees choose their own place to nest.

If however you want to engage the children in the wonderful world of the solitary bees and you want to support and help the bees too, then save up and invest in a specially designed bee box that can be opened and cleaned, and offers an observation window into the world of the developing bee. It might cost more than you planned to spend, but it can be managed and reused for many years. The award winning 'Nurturing Nature Solitary Observation Nest Box' (*Ref 77*) is an excellent design. Made from timber, it's inspired by nature and driven by science. Wildlife World makes interactive solitary bee houses with stacking trays that can be opened and cleaned.

If you want to buy a nest box for solitary bees where you can watch the bees nest and the larvae develop, consider a timber observation nest box from Nurturing Nature.
© *Jean Vernon*

THE FLOWER BEES

There are five species of flower bee in the UK all belonging to the genus Anthophora. They are a similar size and shape to a bumblebee, which can cause a little confusion. But some have very specific behaviour and are fast flyers, darting about, and most have colouring or other identifying features to help you tell them apart.

Hairy-Footed Flower Bee (*Anthophora plumipes*)

This little beauty is one of the earliest garden bees to emerge, sometimes as early as February, and is usually around until midsummer. In the bee world it is the species that heralds the start of spring, emerging when the early spring flowers are starting to blossom.

If you live in the southern half of the UK there's a good chance you will see this bee in your garden, especially in gardens with a rich diversity of spring flowers planted in abundance.

It's a type of solitary bee, and has a few favourite plants that it visits for food, one of which is the early flowering lungwort (*Pulmonaria officinalis*) where it can be found flitting very fast from flower to flower as it feeds.

It's an accomplished aerial acrobat and skilled at hovering, resembling a little hummingbird in its mode of action. It is pretty difficult to photograph because it moves so fast, but that actually helps in identification of this species. If you've got a decent patch of lungwort in flower there's a good chance you'll get the Hairy-footed flower bee visiting. It's widespread, but more common in the south and east England. Records are gradually increasing further north too, but it is currently

The male of the species is a prettier bee than the black female and feeds on nectar-rich spring flowers such as rosemary. © Steven Falk.

unknown in Ireland and Scotland (*Ref 48*). It's more common in Europe where it occurs in different colour forms (*Ref 49*). The Hairy-footed Flower bee is bumblebee shaped; the females are black with gingery hairs on their back legs, the males are a yellowy/ginger/orange colour with a creamy apricot moustache and they have feathery legs. If you are a fan of BBC's *SpringWatch* you might have seen a clip on the programme in 2017 showing these amazing bees. Check out YouTube (*Ref 50*) as there's a clip on there and it's well worth a watch. It's a slightly intrusive insight into the courtship of these little bees and actually takes place on a lungwort flower. The female, who only mates once, is choosy in her choice of parent for her babies. So the male Hairy-footed flower bee has to perform a few acrobatic manoeuvres to win her heart, but he has a surprising bedside manner to add to the equation. Before the courtship, the male not only has to literally hang in the air to win her attention, but he has to move fast to gain his prize before his competitors move in. But while in the act of mating, the male appears to massage her eyes with his feathery front legs. It's a touching display that you may never get to see in 'real life' but you can replay on YouTube if you can find it.

These bees nest in burrows excavated in compacted clay banks, old cobb walls, soft mortar, cavities in soft cliff faces, clay soil (*Ref 51*) and even around weathered chimneystacks. The nests are usually quite shallow, but the bees can nest *en masse*, giving the appearance of a social species, when in fact they are an abundance of solitary bees nesting in aggregation.

Once mated the female returns to her nest where she has made little cells for her offspring. She lays an egg into each cell and provisions it with a ball of pollen, sometimes wetted with nectar. Then she seals the cell. Inside, the egg will hatch into a larva that will eat the pollen and then pupate in the cell to emerge in spring to start the cycle over again.

Like most solitary bees the males emerge first so that they are ready for the arrival of the females. The males hang around the food plants of choice for this species, waiting for the female and seeing off competition. This behaviour is often seen around established clumps of lungwort.

How to spot them
Look out for nest sites in the mortar between the bricks in walls and soil banks. As the weather starts to warm in early spring it is the males that emerge first. They can get quite excited visiting the nest sites where the females are yet to emerge and can be spotted flying into the nests looking for a mate.

The best way to see these bees is to stake out the early spring flowers of lungwort (*pulmonaria*) on the lookout for fast moving, hovering bees, remembering that the black ones are the females and the gingery, feathery legged ones are the males. Start looking in early March when the plants are in flower, but in milder spells they can emerge

A cobb wall made of mud, grit and straw is a perfect place for these bees to nest. © Shutterstock/Ed Phillips

Spring flowers with a deep corolla and nectar reward, such as primulas, are the preferred feeding places for the Hairy-footed flower bee. © Brigit Strawbridge Howard

in February. These bees will also visit other early spring flowers such as comfrey, primroses and dead nettles: all nectar rich blooms and common garden plants.

If you don't have these in your garden, you can visit public gardens and parks and look for them. Make it into a treasure hunt with the kids, take a camera and take lots of photos and try and ID what you see.

The garden at RHS Wisley in Surrey has an aggregation of Hairy-footed flower bees that have nested in a cobb wall on site. The entomologists have created an information board to introduce the visitors to this enigmatic bee. It's a great way to spread the word about solitary bees to the very gardeners that may come across them in their plots.

How to help them

If you've spotted this bee in your garden then submit a report to BWARS so that it can be added to the research on this species. This is especially important as the parameters of the distribution of this bee are still unclear and it is unknown in some areas of the northern UK, Scotland and Ireland.

Plant pulmonarias around your garden; it's a pretty groundcover plant and will help all manner of bees, but is a favourite of this species in particular.

Divide established clumps and pot them up for friends and family so that more people grow it.

Let white, red and spotted dead nettles grow in the wilder parts of your garden.

If you only have pots and containers on a patio or terrace then plant spring primroses and primulas, seeking out those grown organically and without the addition of pesticides. Grow them in a sunny spot.

If you have a grassy bank, plant wild primroses to flower in the spring for an early source of nectar.

Leave old cobb walls and any soft mortar joints between bricks and stones in walls. If you see them nesting there leave them alone to complete their lifecycle. You can also make small blocks or bricks of cobb (clay or soil mixed with grit and straw) and create new habitat as part of an insect house or wildlife shelter.

Leave an area of soil, especially on a bank, as bare soil. If it's a sunny south-facing grassy bank then cut it tight to expose the soil and leave it for the bees to nest. You may not attract Hairy-footed flower bees to nest there, but it's a good habitat for all sorts of other creatures too.

OTHER SPECIES OF NOTE

The Green-eyed flower bee (*Anthophora bimiculata*) is more likely to be seen in southern counties of the UK. You can tell it apart from the Hairy-footed Flower bee because it doesn't have hairy legs, but instead has fabulous pale green eyes and a yellow face.

The Forked-tailed Flower bee (*Anthophora furcata*) is another flower bee you may find in your garden.

This beauty is a Green-eyed flower bee, Anthophora bimaculata. © Steven Falk.

The Nomad Bees *(Nomada species)*

The nomad bees can be found in gardens, parks and in nature in spring. From an amateur's perspective they mostly look more like wasps than bees, with a fairly hairless orange/yellow stripy abdomen. There are 32 species known in the UK and all of these are cuckoo bees of other solitary bee species, which like the bird they are named after, lay their eggs in the nests of their host bee species. This means that the offspring of the host bee in the affected nest will not survive to the next season.

The Flavous and Panzer nomad bee look similar; they are both cuckoo bees of solitary Andrena mining bees. © Jean Vernon

And while that seems very sad, the presence of the nomad bee does indicate a healthy population of the host bee. The two have evolved together through millennia to exist side by side. Without a good host population the associated nomad bee will die out. There are many different cuckoo bees, most are host specific and will only affect nests of particular species. The nomad bees are just one genus that generally affect the mining bees (Andrena species) and are found in spring corresponding to their lifecycles.

The Violet Carpenter Bee (*Xylocopa violacea*)

One of the reasons that the number of bees in the UK varies is because of the occasional arrival of a new bee (as well as very sadly the odd extinction). The Violet carpenter bee isn't new to science but it is relatively new to mainland Britain. Reports of a large blue-black bee, with a metallic blue sheen to the wings, being seen in gardens in the Midlands in 2006 and 2007 were eventually corroborated and confirmed to be the Violet carpenter bee. It's one of Europe's largest solitary bees and was found in sufficient numbers to suggest that it had actually bred in the UK and overwintered. Climate change has enabled this European migrant to not only feed and breed here, but to overwinter too. It might be large and to some people a little scary, but like most solitary bees it won't sting you.

With its blue violet wings and the fact that it nests in old timber and especially old and dead wood trees, it lives up to its name in every way. Like the hummingbird hawk moth, another European migrant, we can expect to see more of this beautiful, large black bee in our summer gardens.

If you've spotted a large, shiny black bee around the flowerbeds then it could be the Violet carpenter bee.
© Shutterstock/Eileen Kumpf

How to spot

If you see a huge, shiny black bee in your garden then it's pretty likely to be the Violet carpenter bee. Report your sighting to BWARS or another wildlife recording site and try and get a photograph for confirmation.

It's bigger than a queen bumblebee and it is quite loud as it forages for food. Check it out on YouTube and watch its metallic wings shimmering in the sunlight as it forages for food on thistle flowers.

How to help

Be observant. If you can trace the adult bees to a nest then that would be useful information for one of the entomology departments at a museum or university. Take pictures. Notice what the bees are feeding on. General reports are that it forages on many garden flowers, including lavender and cirsium.

Leave old trees to decay naturally to provide nesting sites for beetles and other mini beasts.

HONEYBEE (*APIS MELLIFERA*)

If you mention the word bee or declare an interest in these little creatures, the conversation almost immediately turns to honeybees. But honeybees are just one species of the 276 other species that we are blessed with in the UK.

Many people get interested in wild bees through conventional beekeeping and that's a good place to start. But it's important to remember that most honeybees are domesticated and whether there is such a thing as a wild colony is a hotly contested topic. However, what is clear is that honeybees can and do survive without the care of a beekeeper as a feral colony. And there are many honeybee colonies of significant age living undisturbed in house roofs, hollow walls, chimneys and even beneath floorboards. The very existence of these established colonies sheds light on a belief by natural beekeepers (*Ref 52*) that bees can rise above some of the pests and diseases that they are plagued by in domesticated hives, and in particular the varroa mite.

Wild honeybees can and do exist without the care and management of beekeepers, and while some regard these colonies as disease ridden, others see the beauty and value of these independent pioneering survivors. For these bees have learned how to deal with the pests and diseases and the dreaded varroa mite without any assistance. In this way, the survival of the fittest 'wild bees' may in fact pave the way for healthier strains of these rightfully revered creatures.

Honeybees in the Garden

An understanding of the needs of honeybees traverses into the world of bumblebees and solitary bees too. There is nothing wrong in keeping bees, but be clear why you

A clustered swarm of honeybees is simply waiting for the colony to decide which new home is the most suitable for their needs. © Jean Vernon

There are dozens of different types of bee hive used by beekeepers all over the world. Each one provides the bee colony with a place to live. © Martin Mulchinock

want to do so. Is it for the bees or is it for the honey? If you want to keep bees for the sake of the bees remember that keeping honeybees will not save bees. It's a bit like keeping chickens to save wild birds (*Ref 53*). But if you choose to care for a colony of honeybees with their interest at heart in a bee-centric way, now referred to as natural beekeeping, you will find a band of others with similar ideals to support and advise you. If you simply want the honey, then remember that this can be a time consuming, costly hobby, that while very fulfilling, it carries with it some serious responsibilities. It's nothing like keeping a cat or a dog and will demand your undivided attention at the drop of a hat or the appearance of a swarm.

If you are ever lucky enough to witness the arrival of a swarm you are extremely privileged and the memory will stay with you forever.

A swarm cluster can hang for a few hours or even a few days. These precious creatures face such monumental challenges that every swarm needs a rescue package, and only a quarter of swarms survive in the wild. Now is the time to call for a beekeeper, preferably one that nurtures the natural behaviour of bees, otherwise known as a natural beekeeper. But any local beekeeper can offer expert advice and hopefully assistance in an emergency.

Exploding Genitals

On a still summer's day the new virgin honeybee queen bee who has emerged in the parent hive, will risk her life on the most important flight of her life: her marriage flight. She will fly high to an area called the drone congregation zone, where male bees (drones) gather together. They are waiting for a queen to chase and mate with. It is the fastest, fittest males that will succeed in passing on their genes (and the genes of the queen that laid their egg) to future fertilised eggs in the new colony that will grow into queens or worker bees. In effect the male bees are flying sperm, for they only carry the genetics of their parental queen. The male bees die immediately after mating; the process is pretty violent and actually explodes their genitalia with force, ultimately resulting in their death.

CHAPTER THREE

Bee Behaviour

The more you watch and observe bees of all types the more you will learn about these complex, delicate and amazing creatures. Each species is different and many have very idiosyncratic behaviour. Here are a few of the things you might notice or want to learn a little more about.

Bees Need Water

Even though bees drink and collect nectar they also need to drink water. Rainwater is better for them than tap water and you can easily provide a safe bee drinker for bees in your garden with a shallow bowl filled with marbles, glass beads, or pebbles topped up with rainwater. Bees will stand on the protruding objects and use them as safe islands to drink from. If you have a bird bath or a pond you may find struggling bees that have fallen in, or worse those that have drowned; a shallow area of pebbles will help them drink safely and escape and is also suitable for other wildlife to enter and leave.

Bees use water for lots of reasons. In the heat of the summer they will evaporate water inside their nest or hive to reduce the temperature. In early spring a colony of honeybees may use water to release honey in their stores that has crystallised over the winter.

Bees will also visit open, deep water, so keep a watch and if they choose something other than your bee drinker, provide a platform for them to drink from by floating sticks or corks there or placing rocks in the shallows.

Make a bee drinker in the garden where insects can reach the water without drowning. © *Martin Mulchinock*

The Sting

Bees do sting and yes sometimes it hurts. Solitary bees do have stings but most are not strong enough to pierce our skin and so these bees are considered to be safe for children and pets.

This bee isn't waving hello – it's telling you to back off. © Jean Vernon

Bees don't usually sting without reason. They usually give you a warning and if you don't read the warning and back off then they may well attack. Honeybees will buzz loudly at you or even bounce off you before stinging. Bumblebees will do a 'high-five' manoeuvre and wave a back leg at you; you might see this if you get too close with a camera.

But unless you interfere or endanger a bee nest, most of the time the bees are just going about their business and won't take much notice of you. The actual mechanism of the sting is an adaptation of the female egg laying tube (hence why only the females can sting) and even queen bees have the capacity to administer a painful attack.

It's worth remembering that honeybees and only honeybees usually die when they sting because their sting is barbed and they leave it in the victim with a venom sac still pulsating and pumping poison. Other bees don't do this and can sting again. Remember that most bees are not aggressive and will only sting when threatened or when protecting their nest.

Solitary Bees are Safe for Children

Solitary bees can sting but rarely do and when they do it's nothing like the biological warfare effect of a honeybee or bumblebee sting. Sometimes it's just a little nip and most of the time you would barely notice. Some of the male solitary bees have spiky bottoms, which they use to protect their territory and their female from other bees, but again these would rarely be used against people, and remember male bees can't sting.

Mason bees don't sting or spike and this makes them a particularly good choice for educating children. Mason bees are some of the bees that will build a nest in a bee house and are excellent pollinators too.

Avoiding Stings

Tread gently around bees, especially near their nests, and don't wave your arms about or swat them away.

If picking flowers, make sure there is not a bee inside the blooms as you pick.

Teach children to treat bees with respect and care.

Some people are seriously allergic to bee stings and can go into anaphylactic shock after a sting. Don't delay in seeking emergency medical attention if anyone has breathing difficulties or a bad reaction to a sting.

Some health therapists use bee sting acupuncture to treat chronic and autoimmune diseases, but it is a very controversial therapy and not widely used.

Massive Attack

If you get stung by one bee, be careful, there's a good chance if you hang around you'll get stung again. That's because when a social bee attacks and also when it dies it releases a pheromone, a message smell that tells the other bees, so they will also attack and sting. This is what happens when someone is stung badly. If a honeybee stings you then you need to scrape off the sting without squeezing it. A sharp nail dragged sideways across the sting, which will protrude from your skin, will remove it without pushing any remaining venom into your system. The sting will pulsate even after it has been deployed so getting it out fast will help lessen its effect.

If you have an allergy to stings seek medical advice immediately and advise someone nearby that you have been stung so that they can get help. Most people aren't allergic, but that doesn't mean that it won't hurt. Bee venom is used as a treatment for several conditions. It is controversial but has been used by MS sufferers with some success. This type of treatment is called Apitherapy.

Male Bees Can't Sting

It's only the female bees that can sting, so if you learn to identify the male bees correctly you can in fact pick them up very gently without the risk of a barb. It's a good 'party trick' but only if you know what you are doing – don't do this if you don't.

Learn to identify the male bees; they don't collect pollen so they don't have pollen baskets on their legs. For solitary bees check whether they have pollen brushes.

It is safe to gently pick up and examine a male bee because they are unable to sting you, but you need to be able to tell the males from the females. © *Jean Vernon*

Male bees have 13 antennae segments compared to the female's 12 (you can use a magnifying lens to count them) but sometimes the antennae are obviously longer.

They are not usually rushing about foraging frantically, instead lingering on a nectar flower at the proverbial bee-nectar bar. Male solitary bees are also often slimmer and less colourful than their female counterparts.

Bumblebee Male Bees Have Facial Hair

Weirdly and quite amusingly male bumblebees also often have facial hair, usually yellow or cream in colour and very moustache like. Like many bee species their prime interest is meeting and mating with a female of its species. The bright moustaches are thought to be a way of communicating sexual prowess to the females and that the queens select accordingly.

Look closely and you can see this bee has a yellow moustache, which helps identify it as a male. © Jean Vernon

The males don't collect pollen, simply feeding on nectar to sustain themselves, and can often be found in number hanging out outside a nest waiting for the females to emerge or overnighting in a flower close to its food source, a bit like a nectar bar. Males aren't usually in a hurry, except when there is a female about, and so often when feeding they appear to move over the flower feeding as they go and perhaps enjoying the vibe!

These behaviours are all ways to help identify the males from the females.

Buzz Pollination

Most garden bees buzz making a rich resonating sound in our gardens. It's the sound of summer and wonderful noise. Some bees are louder than others, such as the queen Buff-tailed bumblebees, which sound like a low flying helicopter when they whizz over your head. The Shrill carder bee has a slightly higher pitched buzz giving it its common name. But stand beside a rose bush or poppy flowers in summer and you can hear the unmistakable sound of a bumblebee working the pollen inside the flowers. A higher pitched buzz is a technique that bumblebees use to extract pollen from particular flowers where the pollen is packed tightly in the anthers and harder to get out. It's called buzz pollination or sonication.

Listen out for the higher pitched buzz of bumblebees in certain flowers, particularly poppies, where the bees need to raise the frequency to release the pollen. © Brigit Strawbridge Howard

The bee grabs hold of the anthers with its legs and contracts its flight muscles to vibrate the anthers to a higher frequency which releases the pollen in a shower that then sticks to its body. It's an essential method of pollination for tomato plants, which is why bumblebees are sold commercially to tomato growers for use in vast glasshouses.

Some solitary bees are also able to buzz pollinate.

Smelly Bees

Bees smell and use smells to communicate with each other. Generally we can't actually perceive the smell, but the finely tuned pheromones that create the bee smells are extremely important to the bees.

Male bumblebees scent mark leaving little postcards of information for queen bumblebees in places they frequent.

Male bees emit strong sex pheromones to attract females and if you catch them sometimes you can actually smell their scent close up. Close observation of male bumblebees by Bumblebee Conservation Trust officers (*Ref 54*) has revealed that different species emit a different kind of perfume. Captured inside a marking cage or magnifying pot the males release a whiff of pheromones, which to the human sense of smell resembles citrus in the case of Red-tailed bumblebees, and a more cheesy, smelly feet smell from the Early bumblebees.

These pheromones are species specific to ensure that the males attract the females of their species.

Smell and Taste

Bees use their antennae to smell and taste, waving them in the air to pick up the finest whiffs of pheromones and floral scents and to ascertain the quality of nectar. They don't want to waste time collecting poor quality nectar if there's something better available. Let's face it, if you could dine in a gourmet restaurant instead of a cheap eats outlet without costing you any more, you would. So if the bees can find fine dining as fast and as near to their nest they will always choose that over a weaker, more dilute offering of nectar.

Calling Cards

Dave Goulson tells of bumblebees leaving messages to others that they have visited particular flowers (*Ref 55*). This explains how bees know what flowers not to visit and helps to save vital energy as they forage for food. He reports bumblebees having smelly feet and leaving traces of pheromones on the flower petals as they move from bloom to bloom.

Recent research (*Ref 56*) from the University of Bristol in the UK discovered that bumblebees can tell the difference between the scent of different bees and that they use this to help them find good sources of food and to avoid flowers that have already had their nectar taken. The bees secrete markers when they land on a flower, a bit like a finger print, and it is the whiff of these that informs the bees of any recent visits. Most flowers replenish their nectaries to attract pollinators and the scent marks fade over time, so that a flower visited some time ago becomes again attractive to foraging bees. Researchers think that this could help the bees remember or at least identify which flowers they have visited recently too. There is also an electrical field around flowers that is altered when a bee visits, and some flowers, such as borage, rather conveniently change colour when they have been pollinated and stop producing nectar.

Mini Bees

Look out for pea-sized bees early in the bee season, in May. These are usually the first brood bees from a bumblebee nest though they can also occur later in the season.

The queen bee has a lot to do to raise the first worker bees and she has to do it all on her own, so it's no surprise that sometimes the first brood of bees that hatch are a bit malnourished and small. Sometimes they might have been at the edge of the brood chamber and just not got the food when she brought it back. Once the new workers take over, pollen and nectar are brought back to the nest regularly so there's plenty of food and the next generations are bigger than the early mini bees. Bumblebees use two different methods of storing and feeding the brood once the workers take over. Some like the Common carder bee and the Garden bumblebee make little storage pockets out of wax in the nest and the larvae compete for the contents, meaning some are well fed and others less so. The other bees, which are considered to be more advanced (Ref 57) feed the larvae one by one as they return to the nest, resulting in more uniform sized bees. These bees also store excess pollen in wax pots like urns (think 'Winnie the Pooh' honey pots) that act as a reserve of food when bad weather stops the bees from going outside.

The good thing is that the little bees are better foraging in hot weather as they have a greater surface area to lose heat and they can move a bit faster. The bigger bees are better in colder temperatures and can carry a bigger pollen load. That's why on very hot days you might not see the larger bumblebees out and about in your garden. And of course the plants don't produce as much nectar when the ground is dry and it hasn't rained for a while.

Food Rationing

Solitary bees, honeybees and some bumblebees are very particular in how, when and where their offspring are fed, provisioning each egg and developing larva with just the right amount of pollen to mature.

THE SECRET LIVES OF GARDEN BEES

Most bumblebees are a little more haphazard and this is reflected in the development of the brood.

Worker bumblebees bring pollen and nectar back to the nest and deposit it within the brood chamber. The larvae nearest this point get the most food and will grow into the biggest bees, any on the periphery get what's left and these bees will be smaller. This means there will be a mix of different sized bees from one bumblebee nest.

When honeybees bring food back to the colony it is taken inside by worker bees that distribute it to nurse bees that are feeding the young.

Royal Perfume

The queen bumblebee releases a pheromone inside her nest that communicates a kind of 'all is well' smell to keep the workers calm and content and fully operational, it's essential for the well-being of the nest. If the queen bee dies and this scent wears thin, the workers may actually start laying eggs and chaos takes over the colony until it eventually dies out.

In a healthy colony, inside the bumblebee nest around mid summer the queen lays a batch of unfertilised eggs that will develop into strong young males of the species. In effect the male bees don't have a father, but they do have a maternal grandfather. The male bees carry the genes of their mother, the queen bee. All female eggs are fertilised.

The queen will also lay a cluster of new queen bee eggs that will emerge as virgin queens. Once this is done and the young males and queens become adult and go out to mate, her job is done; she has populated the local environment with a fresh generation to continue the species and her pheromone inside the nest fades. The workers lose their instructions and the nest is reduced to chaos. The pheromone scent is what holds it all together, and gradually the colony dies. Of course all is not lost because the new mated queens will hopefully survive to continue the lifecycle.

Bee Love

Garden bees have various ways of finding their mate and their courtship activities can be at very different times of the year.

The honeybee queen needs a sunny day for her marriage flight and will leave the hive and fly to what is called the drone congregation zone, basically an area chosen by the males where they hang out and wait for their queen.

Bumblebee males have different ways of finding their partner. It is the male bees that stake out an area, sometimes at the top of a hill and sometimes along a hedge, spotting their pheromones occasionally as little post-it notes for the queen bumblebee to find. Charles Darwin spent periods studying bees and the behaviour of male bumblebees and encouraged his children to find and follow the paths of male bumblebees in his garden at Down House in Kent (*Ref 58*).

In summer when the new daughter queens of the Great yellow bumblebee emerge they quickly mate with male bees of their species before they feed up and get ready to overwinter. © BBCT/Gordon Mackie

Other bumblebees have a territorial route at tree level with a regular fly past searching for their mate. Bumblebee queens mate a few days after they emerge in summer. They can mate once or a few times, but in some species the male bee actually leaves a plug inside the female bee after mating to stop another male from mating with her, this breaks down after a few days and so the female can mate again.

Bumblebees usually mate on the ground or on a hard surface and you may observe this behaviour while out in your garden.

Gangs and Nectar Louts

Male bees have one main purpose in life and that is to find a mate. Bumblebee males, once they emerge from their nest, do not return and are not usually allowed back in. They generally emerge before the daughter queen bees from their own nest and start to disperse looking for a mate. This means they are less likely to mate with their sisters. Male bees don't collect pollen as they don't feed the babies and instead hang about in the flowers, like fluffy lager louts, supping nectar and waiting for the girls. As they can't go back 'home', male bees will actually sleep overnight inside flowers and can be found early in the morning, motionless waiting for the sun to warm them up. There is even a solitary bee, *Chelostoma florisomne*, whose name translates to Flower Sleeper and may be found inside buttercups (*Ref 59*) in bad weather, sheltering inside as the flowers close.

Side by side these male bees feed apparently contentedly, and yet the bee on the right, Bombus sylvestris is a male of the species that destroy the other bee's offspring. @ Jean Vernon

Once active, male bumblebees will patrol an area on the lookout for a mate and paint patches of their pheromones at points on their route to leave messages for passing queens. They secrete these pheromones from near their face and use specially adapted hairs to brush them onto stems and branches where their potential mates may fly. When a queen bee of the same species passes by and shows an interest it ensures that the male bees mate with the correct species and don't waste time pursuing a female from another clan.

Bees See in Ultra Violet

Take a look at the colour range of the plants that you most frequently see bees feeding on and you might be surprised at the spectrum of colours. Bees don't see colours like we do. Their vision is within the UV spectrum and this gives them extra sensory powers when it comes to seeing things. Flowers that we see in full technicolor are seen very differently by a bee. They have compound eyes. They can't see red, it looks black

Some flowers like this cranesbill have very obvious guidelines for bees to find the nectar. © Jean Vernon

to them. But they can see green and blue and UV light which illuminates the lines on the flowers that are often invisible to us that guide them to the nectaries. These petal markers absorb UV light and create patterns visible to the bees.

Have a little fun this summer and start to record not just which flowers the bees visit in your garden, but the colour of the flowers they choose to feed on.

Some research (*Ref 60*) suggests that purple flowers, often the preferred colour of many bees, have more nectar, with blue flowers a close second. There is also some evidence (*Ref 61*) that suggests flowers and flower colour have evolved to suit the colour vision of the native bees. But remember that many of our garden plants are not UK native and hail from far distant shores.

Winter Active Bees

While most wild bees are either overwintering in nests, insect houses or hidey-holes for the winter, or hunkered down in the hive (honeybees) to weather the cold, sometimes on sunny days you might find a bumblebee out in the garden. This unusual behaviour is becoming more common and is thought to be a result of climate change.

Bumblebees are more resilient to cold weather than most bees; they have a hairy coat that traps air and provides insulation, and some species like the aptly named *Bombus polaris* are even found above the Arctic Circle (*Ref 62*). Queen bees are able to withstand extreme temperatures during their winter torpor.

But it is the bumblebee's ability to regulate their temperature by disengaging their wings and vibrating the muscles in their thorax to heat themselves up that allows them to get going in cooler temperatures. This means that they can and do start flying earlier in the day so that they can beat other bees to nectar sources, and they can also fly in cooler temperatures.

Usually bumblebees overwinter as mated queens and although occasionally one may emerge on a warm sunny day in winter, it doesn't explain the presence of worker bees in winter. There is now evidence that some daughter queen bumblebees that emerge from the nest in summer and mate may go on to make a nest that same summer rather than overwinter, thus creating winter active bumblebees. This may explain why in milder spells and on sunny winter days, worker and male bumblebees have been spotted feeding on nectar-rich winter flowering plants. Keep a look out in your garden in winter and see what you can find foraging on your winter flowers. Generally it is just the Buff-tailed bumblebees that are thought to exhibit this behaviour in some of the warmer parts of the UK such as southern England and south Wales. Look out for the bees in public parks densely planted with winter bedding and flowering shrubs and also in your garden. Sightings should be reported to BWARS (*Ref 63*) and the BBCT to extend the information available about this behaviour. Take photographs if you can to verify dates and help identify the species and the plants they are feeding on. It's another reason to make sure that your garden has flowers all year round, but especially over the winter months.

CHAPTER FOUR

Bee Food

The main reason bees visit flowers is not to effect pollination, it is predominantly to feed, although there is also some evidence that they also 'self medicate' by feeding on nectars rich in specific compounds that have a medicinal effect on the bees themselves (*Ref 64*).

In simple terms bees and other insects harvest nectar from flowers as an energy-rich fuel to keep them alive. It is also used to wet pollen, making it stick to the bees pollen baskets and in some species, mostly bumblebees, it is stored in little 'Winnie the Pooh' shaped honey pots to sustain the queen while she sits on her first brood of eggs, and as an energy source for bad weather.

In the UK it is *only* the honeybee that processes nectar into honey and stores it for its winter food.

A sneak peek inside a bumblebee nest where there's a jumble of waxy cocoons attended to by the worker bees.
© *Jean Vernon*

Nectar, usually described as a high energy, rich in carbs, food for bees (and other pollinators) is more than just a sugary substance. It contains different forms of sugar: glucose, fructose and sucrose, but it also contains a wealth of other ingredients, including a diverse mix of constituents with a range of unseen benefits, including antioxidants and potential antimicrobial action.

The quality and quantity of nectar varies depending on the plant species, the pollinator it is attracting, the time of year and even the weather.

Flower Essences

Do bees gather this nectar because it is good quality food to sustain their activity, or because it contains powerful antimicrobial and antifungal properties? Do they sup nectar from herb plants when they are ailing, in the same way that animals graze on herbs when they are unwell? Some research suggests that they do.

Thanks to Dr Edward Bach and his Bach Flower Remedies, there is vast interest in the use of plant essences for healing the emotions. Whether you believe in this or not, it's curious to wonder whether the bees too obtain more than just food for sustenance when they collect their flower food. Do the flower essences provide nurture for the soul? And do the bees also choose flowers for their essences and medicinal properties as well as the quality of the nectar?

If we consider the medicinal properties of herbs that we use and revere, they are powerful ingredients in our diets and health. In the same way there is a good chance that these properties are also present in the nectar and pollen of the herb plants. This is collected by the bees to be added to the nectar stores and pollen bread that they make for their offspring. Thyme plants are popular food plants for all sorts of bees, their tiny tubular flowers are an excellent source of nectar. Researchers from the University of Massachusetts (Ref 65) have recently helped to show that thymol, a metabolite found in thyme nectar, is biologically active against some bee gut parasites. Bees infected with certain parasites have actually been shown to spend longer foraging on plant species offering these medical properties, returning to forage on that plant species more often. Whether the bees know, and if so how do they know that these plants are good for them is unclear, as is the method of sharing and passing on this information.

More scientific research by Dartmouth College (Ref 66) has discovered bumblebees carrying some common gut parasites foraging on plants whose nectar and pollen has known medicinal effects. Previously the researchers had discovered in lab research that treating parasitised bees with nectar containing known natural chemicals, including nicotine, significantly reduced the number of parasites in sick bees. The follow-on study shows parasitised bees feeding on plants with secondary metabolites in their floral nectar in higher numbers than healthy bees, suggesting that bees may be able to self-medicate and that they alter their foraging behaviour when loaded with parasites to maximize feeding on plants with seemingly beneficial secondary

metabolites (*Ref 67*). The bees were also more likely to return to these plants to feed and that this in turn resulted in better pollination of the plants, illustrating the delicate and complex relationship between some bees and the plants they pollinate.

Pollen as Bee Food

Pollen is the male gamete of a plant, equivalent to the sperm in animals.

It is produced by the plants, held on anthers, surprisingly rich in protein and is collected and processed by the bees to feed their developing larvae.

For honeybees it is stored in wax cells within the nest and mixed with nectar/honey and other ingredients and fermented into a beebread that is fed to the developing bees. Solitary bees (similar to single mothers) make a ball of pollen wetted with nectar and place this next to each egg they lay to provide food and sustenance for the developing larva.

Bumblebee queens make a large ball of pollen for their first brood of eggs to feed on as they are incubated; after this point it is the worker bees that collect pollen for the subsequent generations.

Pollen is a vital ingredient in the diet of young bee queens. The adult female solitary bees and the new queen bumblebees also need a good supply of protein-rich pollen to

Bees collect pollen to feed to their developing larvae. It's rich in protein. This Buff-tailed bumblebee has a huge load, wetted with nectar in packed pollen baskets. © Brigit Strawbridge Howard

mature their ovaries to start producing eggs. This is why pollen-rich plants, such as sallow/willow are essential in early spring as these bees emerge from their winter torpor.

It is the process of collecting pollen by the bees that makes them good pollinators, though not every creature that visits a flower is strictly a pollinator, and some are more efficient at pollinating than others.

Many solitary bees such as the iconic Leaf-cutter bee have a feathery layer (scopa) beneath their abdomen and as the female bee moves between the flowers she gathers pollen on her underside.

It's a messy process, making these bees and others with a similar hairy chest, very effective pollinators.

From a flower's perspective the messier the bee the better the pollination. This Leaf-cutter bee is covered with pollen. © Brigit Strawbridge Howard

THE BEST POLLINATORS

Many solitary bees collect dry pollen and can get covered in pollen in the process. As they move from flower to flower, the grains are moved around, aiding plant pollination. This makes them better pollinators than most social bees, including honeybees, which collect wet pollen and pack it into pollen baskets. It's a tidier process and so less pollen is lost. If it's better pollination that you need or want, divert your attention to supporting the wild bees rather than deciding to take up beekeeping.

Pollen for Pollination

Pollen is very complicated. To the naked eye it's a powdery, yellow or orange material found on the anthers of flowers. Pollen grains themselves are quite fascinating, especially when viewed under an electron microscope when their shape and form are revealed.

The pollen from each plant type is unique to that species; it's a bit like a fingerprint that's required to open a security door and pretty much only the pollen from the same plant species can pollinate plants of the same or very closely related plants. The pollen has to be compatible or pollination just won't occur. It's a bit like a jigsaw piece fitting into its place on the jigsaw, the right pollen needs to be the correct shape to fit into the female plant parts and trigger pollination. Once in place the pollen actually germinates and transfers the male genetic material to the female ovule where fertilisation occurs.

Wind pollinated plants, where the pollen is carried on the breeze, produce vast amounts of lightweight pollen that becomes airborne and is literally blown around, but only a small percentage will reach female flowers on adjacent related plants. Plants that are wind pollinated include hazel, birch and sweet corn.

Wind pollination is pretty wasteful in terms of pollen, because only a few pollen grains will ever reach their target; the rest will be lost on the wind. Nevertheless these pollen rich plants do provide a useful source of protein for early emerging bees.

Plants that need insects to effect pollination use a wide range of fascinating techniques to attract, lure and control pollinating insects, and especially bees.

These plants generally produce less pollen, with grains that are heavier and stickier so that they are easier to collect. But there are other forces at work too. Bees are generally positively charged and the flowers and plants often have a negative charge, the result being that the pollen and even the flower itself is actually attracted to the body of the bee when it flies into the electrical field. This is most effective when the bees are hairy, and the bee will transfer the 'collected' pollen from flower to flower. The flowers need to make sure that the pollen-covered bees visit flowers of the same type to ensure pollination and to do this they have evolved many incredible tricks and techniques, some of which are so extreme, it's hard to believe they are a result of evolution.

The colourful petals of this eschlotzia are an advertisement for passing bees, promoting the protein-rich pollen.
© Brigit Strawbridge Howard

POLLEN LOAD

Male bees don't collect pollen, so if you see a bee of any type with a pollen load it will be a female worker bee, a female solitary bee or a queen bumblebee. And when the worker bees are collecting pollen it means that there is brood to feed. This protein-rich food is used to feed developing bee larvae.

Electric Attraction (Pollen Magnet)

The fluffy nature of some bees literally attracts pollen to them as they forage; even the male bees will have a light pollen dusting despite not actively collecting pollen. As they move from flower to flower these minute grains are brushed past and onto the sticky stigmas of other flowers.

But it seems that there's some other fascinating bee-flower interactions going on, revolving around a flower's electric aura. Researchers from the University of Bristol (*Ref 68*) discovered, by using fake electrified flowers, that bumblebees can actually

The hairy bodied bumblebees can get covered in pollen as they forage within dense flowers such as this cardoon.
© Jean Vernon

This Leaf-cutter bee pushes into the flower, under the stigma which passes over the bee and collects loose pollen grains from the previous flower it visited. © Jean Vernon

perceive the electrical field around a flower. But they also discovered that the bees seemed to be able to tell which flowers had recently been visited (and the pollen collected or nectar supped) and move to flowers that were unvisited, all through interpreting the electrical fields and the messages they conveyed. It is almost like a note on the door telling the bee whether the flower is open for business or not. We already know they may scent mark flowers as they forage.

Plant pollen is rich in protein to sustain the pollen-eating insects that feed inside the flowers and transfer the sticky pollen to the receptive stigma. Many plants have evolved with and for their insect pollination partners, the flowers acting like flags advertising the whereabouts of essential pollen and nectar. But some have patterned petals with guidelines to direct the bees to the nectar in a path that usually brushes past the pollen-laden anthers, transferring the pollen onto the waiting stigma. This controlling behaviour of plants can be seen throughout the plant kingdom with some quite incredible examples.

Pollen Baskets

Many bees such as bumblebees and honeybees are described as having pollen baskets on their rear legs. Rather than actual baskets, there is a depression in the rear leg structure that is concave and surrounded by bristles.

When the bee becomes covered in pollen it carefully grooms the pollen particles off its face and body, wets them with a little nectar and transfers them to these 'baskets'. A fully loaded bee can carry more than 75 per cent of its body weight in pollen.

A lack of pollen baskets can be useful when trying to identify different bees. Male bees don't collect pollen, so they don't have these pollen baskets. Cuckoo bumblebees don't collect pollen because they rely on the workers of the nest that they infiltrate to provide this protein-rich food for their offspring, so even queen cuckoo bumblebees (there are no workers) don't have pollen baskets.

Specialist Feeders

If life wasn't tough enough for the bees anyway, these little creatures have evolved with different foraging habits. Some bee feeding preferences are dictated by the length of their tongue. For instance, the short-tongued bees just can't reach the deep nectar inside many tubular flowers. But, some bees have found a way to circumnavigate this

Once it has chewed a hole above the nectary of the flower, the bee pokes its long tongue into the hole to soak up the nectar. © Jean Vernon

problem and have become adept at nectar robbing or larceny where they chew a hole adjacent to the nectaries of a tubular flower and then access the nectar.

This isn't good news for the flower as the process bypasses the pollen and anthers and does not effect pollination. But the bees get fast food. It's a cute but sneaky technique and once the holes are present, other bees, including honeybees, exploit the short cut to a quick nectar fix.

The quality and quantity of nectar varies from plant species to plant species and also according to the weather. In hot dry weather nectar production can be affected; conversely after plenty of rain the nectar quality can be diluted. Pollinators such as bees make informed decisions regarding which flowers to visit. They have a technique that they use to tell them if another insect has recently visited a flower; this tells them that it's not worth their effort. But the plants with rich and plentiful nectar will attract more pollinators.

Some flowers, such as borage and penstemons, are credited with dynamic nectar flows (*Ref 69*). Penstemon flowers have been observed to have more than one hundred visits from bumblebees in one day, but the pollen of these plants is released gradually so the plant needs bee visits throughout the day to pick up the pollen as they search for nectar. Some plants are known to replenish their nectaries after the nectar has been harvested several times a day.

Most bees will visit a variety of flowers to sup nectar. Indeed the adults of most bee species appear to survive on a diet of nectar. The males of the species do not collect pollen or nectar for storage and will visit flowers simply to fuel their existence.

Protein

When it comes to pollen some bees are extremely specialist in what they need. Bees that are dependent on a narrow range of plant species for pollen, such as the legumes (pea family), are called oligolectic. A handful of species might depend on just one plant species; these are called monolectic bees and include bees such as the Yellow loosestrife bee (*Macropis europaea*). These specialist-feeding regimes can have dire consequences for the monolectic bee species when the food plant is absent for some reason, or when its flowering period fails to correspond to the lifecycle of the bee.

MONOLECTIC BEES

Some of the monolectic bees in the UK are not monolectic in mainland Europe, where they are known to forage on a wider range of plants. It is not clear whether the bees don't recognise other plant species as being suitable sources of pollen or whether they are so evolved that their larvae cannot digest pollen of different plant species. Whatever the reason it's a classic example of how bees have evolved with our plants and it's remarkable that these bees have survived.

An established meadow, rich in flowers and grasses can support a range of polylectic bees. © Brigit Strawbridge Howard

Bees that can feed from a wide range of plant species are termed polylectic. These bees include the domesticated honeybee and some of the bumblebees. They have the least restrictions on their diet, can visit plants of all sorts for the pollen that they need for their brood and have a better chance of survival because there is less pressure on their food source. Although they have a potentially diverse diet, bumblebees require large areas of suitable habitat to forage efficiently, thought to be in the order of ten square kilometres. The rapid decline in wildflower meadows and suitable habitat has reduced available forage and resulted in the substantial decline of many species.

Lazy Bees

Some bees don't collect pollen even though their brood needs it for its sustenance. Cuckoo bumblebees don't even have worker bees, just females and males. Once successfully mated the female then gatecrashes the nest of a bee of the species she parasitises and lays her eggs in the host nest. She may kill the queen and replace her, but she relies on the worker bees of that nest to raise her offspring. Adult cuckoo bees don't have pollen baskets or queen bees, they simply feed themselves to survive.

Male bumblebees, once they emerge from a nest, do not return and spend their days searching for a mate and drinking bee beer (nectar) from nearby flowers. They do not collect pollen and can often be identified by their behaviour, in that they are often found in or on flowers and rarely seen darting from flower to flower foraging for food. They do not have pollen baskets and can even be found overnighting inside garden flowers.

Poisoned Chalice

Some plants are considered to be poisonous to bees, or the nectar from their flowers creates 'poisonous honey'. This is the case with rhododendron nectar, which contains toxins. Studies carried out at Royal Botanic Gardens, Kew (*Ref 70*) showed that Buff-tailed bumblebees (*Bombus terrestris*), a common visitor to rhododendrons, were not affected by the toxin and it was not repellent or poisonous to them, but honeybees introduced to the toxin died in a few hours. It was also shown to be detrimental to the behaviour of mining bees. The conclusion is that this is yet another highly evolved plant/insect interaction. The toxins are produced by the plants to deter herbivores from eating them, but they also occur in the nectar. In essence it is the pollinators that can tolerate or are not affected by the toxins that will pollinate the flowers. In this instance that means the larger bumblebees, which could spend longer feeding on the flowers and may make more efficient pollinators. Conversely there are some secondary metabolites within other plant nectar that some bees may use to self-medicate.

Other plants have been under suspicion for poisoning bees, such as lime trees (*Ref 71*). Of course trees that are treated by injection against insect pests have and can cause mass deaths of foraging bees. But sometimes the finger of blame gets it wrong.

Rainbow Pollen

When you get used to seeing the bees in your garden, it's great fun to take a closer look at the pollen that they collect on their rear legs. It's always female bees that collect pollen, although male bees can and do get covered in pollen as they forage for nectar.

If you thought pollen was just yellow you might be surprised to learn that it can also be blue, black, dark green, orange, pink, white and grey depending on the flowers it is gathered from.

It's a good way to get the kids involved. Set them a task of trying to see which flowers the bees are visiting and what colour the pollen they are collecting is. You can buy a pollen chart very cost effectively and it's a very useful tool. There are also many resources online.

Some are arranged in seasons and colours so that you can see the colour of the pollen on the bees and look to see what plants they are collecting from. You can

find guides online, but a printed pollen chart is useful to carry around and share with others, and remember that computer monitors display colours in varying degrees of accuracy. You can also use a pollen chart to identify the plants that the bees are visiting and then stake out clumps of the plants to observe the bee activity. This is useful to identify plants that you didn't know were good bee plants, or why your bees aren't visiting the plants that you thought they would, or wanted them to. In effect the bees will visit the plants with the best quality nectar or pollen at that moment in time. So if there is something in flower with better food resources than something else, they will always choose the quality. And of course the more specialist feeders will choose the flowers of the plants that they have evolved with.

Take a closer look at the pollen collected by a bee, it can tell you a lot about the plants that bee is feeding on. © Jean Vernon

Grazers

Generally bees tend to forage on clumps of the same type of flower and gather pollen *en masse*. That's why you see pollen balls of the same colour on the legs of bees. A plant with plenty of flowers offering pollen or nectar is a much more efficient way for a bee to gather food, than flying around, visiting flowers *ad hoc*. It's a bit like comparing the feeding habits of sheep and goats. Sheep graze an area, making the most of the food crop on offer, whereas goats hop about eating pretty much anything and everything in reach.

It is called floral constancy and this is what makes bees great pollinators for crops, because by visiting the same plant species for nectar and pollen for a period of time they will only attract and collect pollen from those plants and transfer it to subsequent flowers of the same species that they visit. To afford pollination the plants' female parts must receive pollen from the same type of flower. So if a bee is specialising in feeding on one species, pollination is much more likely to be effective.

This Common carder bee has hundreds of flowers all in one place to feed on. © Jean Vernon

Talking of Tongues

If you only had a tiny spoon to eat your food it would restrict what you could eat. In the world of bees the shape of the flowers dictates which bees can feed there. While native plants have evolved with the local bees, our gardens actually contain plants from all over the world, including plants that are pollinated in their natural environment by humming birds and other forgotten pollinators. Generally our bees don't really mind that plants aren't native. As long as they are rich in pollen and nectar and the flowers are accessible, the bees will visit. The long tubular flowers of

A long-tongued bee such as this Common carder bee (Bombus pascuorum) can reach into the deep comfrey flowers to feed. © Jean Vernon

plants such as salvias, comfrey and penstemons need the long-tongued bees to visit. Queen bumblebees have slightly longer tongues than their workers, which helps them when nectar rich flowers are sparse; they can visit most flowers that are out in late winter and early spring.

This is clearly shown by red and white clover, a nitrogen-fixing crop that is used as a green manure in agriculture. The seed is collected to sow the crop year-on-year and it requires the pollination techniques of bees.

Honeybees have short tongues, which is why when it comes to pollination the honeybee is not the bee all and end all; they can only pollinate flowers with short floral tubes. Flowers have a huge diversity and require the wide variety of tongue lengths of bumblebees and wild bees to effect pollination. Short-tongued honeybees are excellent pollinators of white clover, which has shorter floral tubes. Only the long-tongued bumblebees can pollinate the longer-tubed red clover flowers.

Don't forget the nectaries are almost always at the base of the flower, which requires the bee to either climb inside the flower, or to poke its tongue into the flower. Bees don't suck up nectar; their tongues soak it up. The length of the tongue dictates what flowers a bee can visit for nectar (see daylight robbery below).

It's the Garden bumblebee (*Bombus hortorum*) that has the longest tongue; it's said to be on average 12mm, but up to 2cm when fully extended. Compared to the size of the bee that's huge. In fact it is so big that the Garden bumblebees fold their tongue

The long-tongued Common carder bee can reach into a flower without climbing all the way in. © *Jean Vernon*

under their head and body, but they can be seen flying with their tongue extended in the vicinity of nectar rich plants.

The Common carder bee has a long tongue, (as do other carder bees), especially compared to its body size.

Daylight Robbery

Naturalist Charles Darwin was possibly the first person to observe nectar robbing by short and medium-tongued humble-bees (as he called bumblebees) (*Ref 72*).

In 1841 in a letter to *Gardener's Chronicle* (*Ref 73*) Darwin wrote about 'the humble-bees which bore holes in flowers, and thus extract the nectar', and speculated about this behaviour as an example of acquired knowledge in insects (*Ref 74*).

He observed the behaviour on garden salvias and penstemons.

In essence, the shorter-tongued bumblebees, namely the Buff-tailed (*Bombus terrestris*) and the White-tailed (*Bombus lucorum agg.*) have developed this devious behaviour. You have to forgive them because when they emerge they need every drop

When a food is scarce some 'clever' short-tongued bees like this Bombus terrestris cheat the plants, bypass pollination and steal the nectar through holes they chew above the nectaries. © Jean Vernon

of nectar they can find, and when it's at the base of a long tubular flower, their short tongues cannot reach it. So they chew, with their mandibles, holes into the base of the flower just above the nectaries. If you look closely at some tubular flowers you can see the holes. It's a common technique on salvias, antirrhinums and comfrey, which normally need a long-tongued bee to pollinate.

The hole is perfectly positioned for the bee to reach inside with its tongue and soak up the nectar. Of course this isn't good news for the plant because it means that the bees bypass the pollen bearing anthers and do not transfer pollen or pollinate the flowers. But it could be a lifesaver for these bees, especially in early spring, when nectar rich flowers are in short supply. Once the holes are in place other nectar feeders will use them to access the nectar, including the short-tongued bumblebees such as the Early bumblebee (*Bombus pratorum*). Honeybees have quickly learned that they can access long tubular flowers via the robbing holes and supplement their diet in this way. This is called secondary robbing because they are looting after the break-in and not actually making the hole.

Plant Resins

There's another ingredient that some bees harvest and use in a variety of ways. It's not exactly a bee food, but it is important. Resin. Remember the sticky buds we picked as children, placed in a milk bottle and waited for the bud to burst? The horse chestnut tree buds, covered in a thick sticky resin?

Well that's just one type of tree that makes a protective resinous layer for its buds. And bees collect these resins. Honeybees mix it with wax and other ingredients and make something called propolis that they use to line the hive and fill in cracks. Beekeepers call it bee glue but it is also revered for its powerful antifungal and antimicrobial properties, to such an extent in that it is harvested and marketed as a healing compound for wounds. Apparently the Egyptians used it to mummify bodies. These days you can buy it in the form of creams, ointments, tinctures and tablets. In the US and Australia there are bees called resin bees, because they use these plant resins when building their nests. Some of our native UK bees also use plant resins: the Yellow loosestrife bee (*Macropis europaea*) uses oil from the flowers to line her nest and waterproof it. We also have a recently recorded resin bee in the UK, called *Heriades truncorum*, or the Large-headed resin bee. It's a type of mason bee, but it's small and can be mistaken for a fly. It uses resin collected from pine trees (*Ref 75*) to seal its egg chambers and the partitions between each cell. It's just possible that this bee was introduced into the UK via imported wood in the Victorian era.

CHAPTER FIVE

The Hostile Garden

Y ou might be surprised to learn that not every plant and its nectar is good for bees
and that there are other dangers lurking in and around your garden.

BEE PREDATORS

Apart from the very recent scare stories about the Asian Hornet (*Vespa velutina*),
which is indeed a serious threat to honeybees, bumblebees and other pollinators, there
is a range of other predators that could be considered a threat to our garden bees.

But put into context with the reminder that nature prevails and most creatures
have a predator of some sort, most of the bee predators have a limited impact on
the wild bee population as a whole, and like the bees that we love and revere, these
creatures also have a part to play in the food chain and the ecosystem. A healthy
population of the bee's parasites, or cuckoo bees, indicates a healthy population of

*The dreaded Asian Hornet has been spotted in the UK in recent years; it is considered a serious threat to honeybees,
bumblebees and other pollinators.* © *Shutterstock/photofort77*

the bees themselves. If the bee species dies out so will its parasite or predator. It's a very delicate balance.

Probably the biggest threat to the bees, and bees of all sorts is man and man's activities. We don't usually eat bees but we can have a huge effect on the survival of wild bees and even honeybees by our behaviour. Loss of suitable habitat for bees to nest and breed is just one of the difficulties facing these sentient creatures. Add to that a lack of suitable food plants corresponding with and correlating to the bee's life cycle, and worse, the application of nerve toxin pesticides to agricultural land and the reality becomes even more apocalyptic for the bees.

But even nature poses a threat in many different ways, with creatures that predate on bees as their own food source and others that will raid a bee nest opportunistically for a rare sweet treat of nectar or the fat, protein-rich babes nestled within the brood nest. But it doesn't stop there. There are mites that feed on the 'blood' of bees, and parasites that do an impersonation of the film *Alien*. And even cuckoo bees that are bees themselves but sneak into a bee nest and lay their eggs in place of their host's eggs and let their host raise their young. It sounds a bit gruesome but it's all part of nature's intricate balance.

Insect Eating Insects

As humans we harness the power of nature in our gardens in a bug-eat-bug philosophy that sees ladybirds and their larvae predating on pesky aphids, and parasitic wasps that can be released into our greenhouses to feast upon whitefly infesting our tomatoes. There are mini beasts that will eat bees, but most creatures leave the bees in peace in fear of their capacity to sting and be stung. A few creatures, such as spiders, will capture or trap bees or other insects to sustain their existence.

Bee Ambush

The Crab spider (*Misumena vatia*) is quite macabre, lying in wait within flowers ready to pounce on the unsuspecting bee (or insect) visitor, which they feed on. They don't make webs but these spiders have crab-like front legs and a skull-like body, but they can actually change colour to camouflage themselves within the flowers, preferring to predate from flowers that are white, yellow or green.

The Crab spider will lay in wait on a flower and pounce on visiting prey. © Jean Vernon

These spiders will take an occasional bee, fly or other insect and don't have a detrimental effect on the bees in your garden. They are fascinating creatures, while a little ghoulish in action, and like all the garden biodiversity should be left to live in peace.

Woven Web Traps

Other web-spinning garden spiders can trap unsuspecting bees in their webs, which they then paralyse and wrap in their silken threads for a meal at their convenience.

Web-spinning spiders lay their sticky traps where insects fly. Once an insect is caught they will string them up for a future meal. © Jean Vernon

Freshly trapped bees can be rescued by breaking the web before the spider reaches its prey, but any bees that have been stunned or ready wrapped by the spider are unlikely to survive and should be left for nature to take its course. Spider webs positioned close to a nest hole, bee colony entrance or even a bee hive could be discouraged manually so that the spider builds elsewhere and doesn't deplete the bee colony in any way at all. But remember that spiders and all other insects are part of the tapestry of life and food for something else. Every creature plays its part in the food chain and the intricate balance of nature, so don't be tempted to disrupt too much, just let nature do what nature does and learn from it.

Bird Snacks

A few birds will eat bees that are walking on the ground and pick them off. Blue tits and great tits are known bee predators but generally not to any great scale. Most birds are wary of the stripy yellow bee uniform, relating it to creatures that are unpleasant to eat or that might sting, but a few will still have a go.

Bee-eaters, not usually native to the UK have recently been spotted in a quarry in Nottinghamshire where they have been seen nesting. In lands where bee-eaters are native, these little birds, as the name suggests, feed on bees. It remains to be seen whether the small population in the UK and repeat visits of these pretty little birds will have an effect on the populations of wild bees that live and nest in close proximity to them.

The bee eater has nested in the UK, but is a relative newcomer to these shores. It feeds on bees and other insects.

Woody Woodpecker

Solitary bees have developed a very clever way to minimise the damage to their next generation during a woodpecker attack. The cavity nesting bees, of which there are many, including those that nest in our bee boxes and insect hotels, lay the precious female eggs at the back of each tube or chamber. The male eggs are laid at the front, and if there is an attack it is the males that are usually eaten. The females deeper inside may well survive, and hopefully there are other males nearby that have not been devoured by the woodpeckers that they can mate with to ensure the survival of the local population. The other reason the males emerge first is so that they can disperse and increase the gene pool in the general population by not mating with their sisters. You can protect your bee box or insect hotel by wrapping it with fine mesh chicken wire that still allows the bees to nest and come and go, but prevents severe woodpecker and other predator damage.

Woodpeckers will also attack surface nests such as those created by the Common carder bee and also the rarer Moss carder bees, Brown-banded carder bee and the very, very, rare Shrill carder bee.

Other Birds

Birds may also access nests of bumblebees for the same reason. Tree bumblebees that nest in bird boxes or tree cavities can also be at risk. It's sad for the bees but the birds need to eat too, so you have to let nature take its course.

Adult bees are not a major food for most British birds, but sometimes blue tits may help themselves to a plump bee to supplement their diet. There have been reports of bumblebees being eaten from the inside out by blue tits and great tits; sometimes the birds peck out the stings and then eat the bees. Research by scientists at the University of Stirling (*Ref 78*) recorded activity at the entrance to 19 bumblebee nests and observed great tits lying in wait at larger nests for emerging bees.

Other incidents of great tits predating bees feeding on rhododendrons (*Ref 79*) and lime trees (*Ref 80 and 81*) have been documented.

Badgers and other Mammals

If you live near woodland or you have a large garden, or even just a garden bordering onto the countryside, you may have badgers nearby. They are nocturnal and an absolute joy to observe, so cat-like and elegant in their movement. But badgers (just like bears) love sweet things and eating grubs. Which means of course that bee nests, especially bumblebee nests, are at risk from their earthly excavations. A badger will seek out an underground bumblebee nest and dig it up feasting on the larvae and any tiny pots of nectar stored in the nest. And given the chance they can also attack a vulnerable honeybee hive, where the prize of a store of honey-packed comb as well as plenty of brood, is of course much bigger, though there are lots more angry bees to contend with. It's rare but it does happen. Hedgehogs may be a predator of ground nesting bumblebees too; they have been observed investigating the entrance holes to nests and even enlarging the entrance on a few occasions when the wild bumblebee nests were being filmed by Stirling University scientists (*Ref 82*).

Mice, shrews and voles are the perfect size to access a bumblebee nest and have been named as predators of bees in literature such as Sladen (*Ref 80*) and were also observed in the Stirling University study.

In fact many queen bumblebees will use any old mouse or vole holes as a suitable nest site. Mice are also a known problem for beekeepers.

Wax Worms

Bumblebee nests can also fall victim to the larvae of the Wax moth (*Aphomia sociella*), which can consume the entire nest, destroying comb and brood. They are also a known problem for honeybee colonies. The adult moths enter the nests and lay their eggs, then the developing larvae feed on the wax comb, destroying the brood of the colony. A wax worm attack can destroy a weak colony, but a strong colony can and will remove the wax worm grubs from a nest.

Bee Parasites

Most creatures have parasites of some sort that can affect them. Honeybees have the varroa mite that can transmit additional diseases to the colony, such as deformed wing virus. Some beekeepers treat their colonies for the varroa mite, introducing

Don't worry too much if you find a bee with mites, usually they are simply hitching a ride from nest to nest.
© Brigit Strawbridge Howard

pesticides into the hive. Natural beekeepers are monitoring treatment-free colonies and have found that the honeybees are learning to deal with varroa mites without chemical intervention. Bumblebees have different forms of parasites. The cuckoo bees which are bees themselves are also true bee parasites, deriving benefits to the detriment of their hosts.

Mites can hitch a ride on a bumblebee and sometimes you find a bee heavy with mites. Generally these are not detrimental to the bee and they drop off in the bee nest, where they devour the nest mess and keep the nest cleaner, hitching a ride out when required.

BEE MIMICS

While out bee spotting in your garden you may well find a number of insects that look like bees but are in fact imposters. There are many. Some mimic the bee's stripy livery to deter predators, giving the impression they will sting or be nasty to eat. Often this gains the mimic a split second advantage, time enough to escape a larger predator. One of these, the Narcissus fly (*Merodon equestris*), is regarded as a pest by some gardeners because it lays its eggs around the base of the dying foliage of daffodils and bluebells and its larvae eat the bulbs. Commercial narcissi growers heat-treat the bulbs to destroy the grubs. It is a hoverfly and as an adult feeds on pollen and nectar, so it's a pollinator that has an important role in the environment.

There are dozens of bee mimics, including this hoverfly known to gardeners as Narcissus fly, as its larvae devour daffodils and other spring flowering bulbs. © Liam Olds

It's no wonder gardeners find bees and insects difficult to identify when there are so many bee mimics to confuse them. This furry hoverfly, Volucella bombylans plumata looks like a bumblebee. © Liam Olds

But some bee mimics use their bee-like appearance as a kind of camouflage to enter the nest of their host species to lay their eggs.

There are bumblebee hoverflies (*Volucella bombylans* and *bombylans plumata*); the former looking like a Red-tailed bumblebee (*Bombus lapidarius*) and the latter with yellow bands and a white tail. They even have a furry body (*Ref 83*) and lay their eggs inside the host bumblebee nest. The resulting larvae will feed on the nest debris and sometimes the bumblebee larvae too.

CUCKOO BEES

There are cuckoo bees for bumblebees and also for many solitary bees. It's a complex subject, but one that needs to be explored. The bumblebee cuckoo bees used to be classified as a different sub-genus (*Psithyrus*) but they are now regarded as bumblebees themselves. Like the cuckoo birds that they are named after, a cuckoo bee will enter a bumblebee nest in late spring or early summer when the worker bees of that colony are gaining strength. The cuckoo bees have species-specific hosts and very often resemble the queen of the host colony, enabling them to enter the nest more easily.

There are no worker bees in the cuckoo bee hierarchy and the adults do not collect pollen, leaving that task to the worker bees of their hosts. The female cuckoo bee, once mated, will hang around feeding on flowers that her host queen bee will visit. When a queen of the correct species feeds nearby she follows her back to the nest where she hangs around outside acquiring the nest scent and presumably biding her time. Cuckoo bees have a tougher exoskeleton and a longer sting than their hosts and when they enter the nest the objective is to kill the existing queen. When she has done that she will then eat the nest eggs and young larvae and lay her own eggs in the nest. These will be raised by the early generations of workers already in the nest and the more mature larvae will grow into the next workers as her larvae develop. Her eggs develop into just males and female queens; there are no workers. When the new cuckoo bee queens and males emerge, the original nest and workers will simply die out and the adult cuckoo bees will leave the nest to start the cycle over again. It sounds pretty

The cuckoo bumblebees are also bumblebee species. Each species has one or two host species whose nests it will exploit, laying its eggs inside where they take over and are fed by the host worker bees. © BBCT/Barbara Grehs

gruesome and in some ways it is, but these cuckoo bees are bumblebees and are only around in any number if their host populations are healthy too.

There are six species of bumblebee cuckoo bees in the UK and some of them are fairly common. They can be difficult to identify, but there are a few giveaways.

First, cuckoo bees don't collect pollen so they don't have pollen baskets on their rear legs. Instead their legs are hairy. They often have dark, smoky glass-like wings and are less active than their hosts as they don't have as much work to do.

THE SECRET LIVES OF GARDEN BEES

CHAPTER SIX

Plant Intelligence

It's not just the bees that have learned over millennia to cheat the plants; some of the plants have evolved some spectacular methods to trick the bees into being better pollinators. Some of these are so extreme and unique it is hard to accept that they are a result of just evolution, and you can't help wonder whether plants also have some kind of intelligence.

FLOWER POWER

My very favourite example of this is a plant I was introduced to at the Alpine house in Kew Gardens in London when I worked there in a summer vacation from university. It was perhaps one of the catalysts to my fascination of bees and plants and has stuck in my consciousness all this time. A small, unassuming little plant that I would have walked past in ignorance, had such a fascinating story and the power to virtually change my life.

The Australian trigger plant is botanically called Stylidium (*Ref 84*). These are rare plants but there are actually over 200 different species in the group, which all use this quite bizarre interaction with their insect pollinators.

I'm not entirely sure which species was growing in the Alpine House at Kew Gardens that summer, but it was a low growing, compact form with pretty pale pink flowers. With the help of a pencil end, which was gently touched into the centre of the flower to mimic a feeding bee, the central trigger, like a tiny pad, whizzes across the flower and hits the visiting bee, either up the bum or between the eyes, depending which way around the bee is facing and the species of the plant. It's fast and fascinating. It's a bit like poking a Venus flytrap to activate the traps, but much, much faster – more like boxing the bee up the bum. There's a clip on YouTube if you want to see it, because of course you can't go around poking plants in botanic gardens. (I was working at Kew in my summer vacation and was being given a guided tour by the Alpine House head gardener at the time!) What's even more fascinating is that the plant can reset itself over the course of ten to twenty minutes. And of course the reason for this mode of action is pollination. Just how this has evolved is beyond me and just proves that plants are far more complicated and evolved than many people think.

The trigger is first bestowed with anthers and pollen and when activated it dusts the bee with the pollen. The anthers deliver pollen to every insect that visits to

If you need a good example of how plants and insects have evolved together in a mutual relationship, take a look at the Australian trigger plant, stylidium. © M.Fagg, Australian National Botanic Gardens

sup its rich nectar and when the pollen has been distributed, then the surface of the trigger plant develops a sticky pincushion of stigmas; the female parts of the flower. Now when an insect stops to drink at its nectar source the trigger cushion, when activated, smacks the bee in the same place, picking up any pollen that has hopefully come from another trigger plant growing nearby. This facilitates pollination bringing the pollen and stigmas of the trigger plants together and forming the seed.

The trigger takes about twenty minutes to reset, but in hot weather when the bees are more active it can reset much faster. It's a fascinating example of a plant taking advantage of bees and one you can read more about online.

Sex Dolls

Other flowers trick insects by mimicking the female of the species so realistically that the lusty males actually try to copulate with the flowers. The Bee orchid (*Ophyrs apifera*) is one of these and it's not just that the flowers resemble the female insect, they can even smell like a female emitting similar pheromones and the flowers are velvety mimicking the feel of a bee. It ends there though and as the male bee tries to mate with the flower, the cunning flower covers it in pollen, which it takes from flower to flower in its quest for love. It's another example of extreme evolution.

How a flower can evolve to not only resemble the female of the pollinating species and smell and even feel like one is quite mind boggling. © Jean Vernon

The Bee orchid grows as a native in the UK and the flowers self-pollinate, so they don't use or need the deception. But in Europe it is our lovely friend the Long-horned bee (*Eucera longicornis*) that is attracted to the bee orchid and assists in its pollination.

Traffic Wardens

Bet you didn't know you'd got floral traffic wardens in the garden (*Ref 85*). Well if you grow foxgloves (*Digitalis purpurea*) you have. They are a great plant to stake out to watch the relationship between bees and flowers in action.

Like most plants, foxgloves 'prefer' to have their flowers pollinated with pollen from other foxglove plants, i.e. not their own. And to ensure that this happens they have evolved some pretty fascinating 'behaviour'. It's hard not to examine this without attributing the plants with some kind of knowledge or brain activity, which of course they don't have. But it does leave you wondering quite how this evolved, or maybe this really is another of God's wonderful creations. Whatever you believe, here is the story (*Ref 86*).

Roadblock

First the foxglove has lots of large flowers on spires and often in great number with many plants in one area. That's great as the plants then stand out like tall pink-purple flags (eye-catching to bees that seem to be attracted by this shade of pink) and attract insect pollinators. The large flowers need a big bee to pollinate them.

Take a close look inside the tube of a foxglove flower and you will see that at the bottom are hairs pointing out of the flower. These are designed to stop small insects, in search of nectar from sneaking into the flower and stealing the nectar without actually effecting pollination.

That's why your foxgloves are a magnet for bumblebees and especially the long-tongued Garden bumblebee. These large bees can climb right into the flowers and as the flower narrows they close their wings as they move towards the nectar prize. As they do so they brush the pollen from the anthers of the flower onto their furry body. Now remember that bees are negatively charged and actually attract pollen to themselves anyway.

Look carefully and you can even see the guidelines to direct the bees to the nectar, which is held at the very top of the flower, deep inside. But this is where it gets very clever. First remember that bumblebees like floral constancy, so they forage on the same type of flower where possible, working the flower patch until they have collected the pollen and nectar on offer. The flowers on a foxglove open at the bottom first. Initially it is the male parts of the flower that mature first and expose the pollen, which then sticks to the bee as it pushes past. The flowers at the top are closed so the bee moves to the next plant. When the male parts of the flower have matured and withered, the female parts mature next, exposing the sticky stigma. Now as the pollen laden large bee arrives from another plant and climbs inside and pushes up towards

Bumblebees are the main pollinator of foxglove flowers, because the flowers have various mechanisms to ensure little insects can't access the nectar. © Martin Mulchinock

the nectar, it brushes past the female parts and any pollen on its body (from previous foxglove flowers and plants) sticks to the stigma of the flower.

Since the flower spike now only has the female flowers at the bottom open, it is more likely that any foxglove pollen that the bee carries must come from another foxglove plant and not from the plant being visited. The flowers at the top of the flower spike will first be male and will open after the female flowers on the same plant have fallen. These have less nectar but are laden with pollen. So the bee is doing a yoyo effect from flower to flower, starting low and moving up and then moving to the next flower when the rest of the flowers are still closed. If there are plenty of foxgloves in an area the bees will visit them in succession and as some flower spikes will be just opening at the bottom with female functioning flowers, others will be almost over with just the male functioning flowers at the top. This clever technique of bee traffic control ensures that the flowers are cross-pollinated with pollen from other plants of the same species. This spreads the gene pool and helps to prevent inbreeding in the species that could result in less vigorous plants.

Bee Trap

Many of the plants that we grow in our gardens hail from far distant shores. In their native land they may be pollinated by creatures we don't have in the UK, such as hummingbirds. These plants will have evolved with their pollinators in the same way that our native plants have evolved with theirs.

One popular garden plant, bear's breeches (*Acanthus mollis*), hails from the Mediterranean and there it is pollinated by large bumblebees.

The bees need to be strong enough to force their way through the cage-like bracts surrounding the flower. It's a stunning plant with fabulous foliage that inspired the

If you grow this common garden plant you may be planting a bee trap for garden bumblebees. © Brigit Strawbridge Howard

Greek sculptor Callimachus (fifth century BCE) to model the capital (crown) of the Corinthian column (*Ref 87*). But it can be a death trap to some of our UK bees. If you grow it, take a close look at the skeleton of the flower when the petals fall and you may well find bee bodies within. It commonly attracts the long-tongued Garden bumblebee (*Bombus hortorum*) to its nectaries; these large bees are strong enough to climb in for the nectar reward, but can't always climb out again, so die inside the cage-like flowers. Potentially the flowers, which bloom in summer, could capture newly emerged daughter queens of nearby colonies that would go on to set up a nest next spring, so these plants could impact on the next generation. If you grow this plant keep an eye on the flowers and release any trapped bees that you find, or if you want to make your garden safer for bees consider removing the flower spikes before they open and grow it for the fabulous foliage instead.

Empty Chalice

Why are lime trees deemed to be the ultimate food tree for bees and yet also responsible for their demise?

It's a very good question and one that has been puzzling experts for many years.

Recent research from Kew (*Ref 88*) has been looking at whether the silver linden tree really is toxic to bees. Rather confusingly the research actually links the mass bee deaths beneath this species of lime to starvation. Not something you would expect when the bees are feeding *en masse* on the lime blossom. But there's much more going on here and plenty more research to be done. The recent research refutes the presence of toxic mannose in lime tree nectar and pollen, which was one suggested cause of the bees' demise. Some bee deaths associated with lime trees have been attributed to treatment of the trees with systemic insecticides (neonicitinoids) to destroy

Despite some concerns, lime flowers are not toxic to bees. © Shutterstock/kosolovskyy

aphids, which have inadvertently killed the feeding bees too. Other suggestions are that something in the nectar is enticing the bees to visit the limes in preference to other forage available but possibly with scant reward and in some cases leading to starvation. It sounds a bit odd, but it seems it is actually the behaviour of the bees that is the issue and that they keep feeding even though the nectar levels are low, then don't have enough energy to return to their nests, resulting in piles of dead bees beneath the trees. It doesn't always happen and it's not toxic nectar, so in essence it is safe to grow lime trees for the bees, but do make sure there are other rich nectar sources available nearby to coincide with the lime blossom.

Plant ASBOs

Then there are the plants that are good for bees, but perhaps, in some opinion, not so good for the garden.

We can argue about whether daisies and clover in the lawn are weeds or wildflowers, personally I favour the latter. If you love bees and pollinators and want to do more for them then you need to rethink your take on weeds. Most plants considered to be weeds are not only good for pollinators and wildlife, but they are also beautiful plants in their own right.

Some of the 'so-called' weeds are so important for early foraging bees that without them the bees (and other pollinators) would be in even more trouble.

Spring Bee Bar

Dandelions are the perfect example of this. These bright cheery yellow flowers are the harbingers of spring. If they weren't such a common plant and already burdened with such negative baggage, then we might actually revere them as a fantastic garden plant. We should, because dandelions are survivors, they colonise bare soil, they flower prolifically and they reseed in cracks and crevices everywhere. Of course you might not want them sprouting up between the paving but these flowers are nothing short of a miracle plant when it comes to the bees and other pollinators. First of all each dandelion flower is not just one flower, it's actually made up of hundreds of individual tubular flowers, each one opening at the top and squashed together to form the perfect dinner plate and landing pad all in one for bees. Our buzzy friends can not only land on the flower, but also move around supping nectar from dozens of flowers in one place. And pollen too. That means there are hundreds of flowers in one place that the bees can feed from without exerting much energy, making the dandelion a very efficient source of bee food. Result. But there's more.

Now remember the first dandelion flowers appear in a warm February and a mild March and then they keep growing and flowering all the way through spring. For early emerging queen bees and foraging honeybees this vital source of nectar provides the perfect fuel to support their foraging, and essential protein rich pollen to

Dandelions might be the only abundant source of food for some pollinators in spring. © Jean Vernon

raise their babes. Be honest and take a look around, there's not much else in flower at this time of year, so rejoice in the presence of these yellow perils and let them grow.

And if that's not enough to persuade you to dump the weed killer and let dandelions grow, think about the other properties of this useful plant. Blanche the leaves by placing a large bucket over a clump or two and you can add the leaves to spring salads. You can eat them green too but they are quite bitter. I am told that if you dig up a few fat dandelion roots and roast them in the oven they make a good coffee substitute. I have to admit I haven't tried that, but I might. And then there's the childhood game of telling the time from the simply beautiful seed heads that scatter in the slightest breath of wind. What you might not know is that there are several seed-eating birds that feed on the copious dandelion seeds produced in spring, so that's another reason to live and let live.

Low Mow

It's time we went low mow or no mow with our lawnmowers, raising the cutting height by 3-4 inches and letting some of these lawn flowers (not lawn weeds) grow. Imagine if every garden owner joined the throng. Then think of the huge mosaic of lawns, from city to country, providing a wealth of nectar and pollen rich flowers for our pollinators. Wow, wouldn't that be a result? We'd have hectares of wildflower-rich forage for bees and other pollinators everywhere and all linked together.

Even if you just let part of your lawn flower, a wide strip, or just alternate the areas that you cut with your mower you can make a huge difference. Or why not just stop mowing from mid May until late summer and see what wildflowers are flowering. Try it, you might decide that you like the effect and you can be sure that the pollinators and bees will find it and show you that they love it too.

Let your lawn grow longer to see what flowers there, and improve its floriferous content by planting wildflower plug plants into the turf. © Brigit Strawbridge Howard

It's not just the rich source of pollen and nectar that will help support the bees. There are many species of solitary bees that make their homes underground; the mining bees and even some bumblebees will make nests in uncultivated soil and lawns, so leaving part of your lawn to nature helps support these bees too.

GARDEN CHEMICALS

If you really want to help the bees and all the other wildlife in and around your garden one of the most effective things you can do is to stop using pesticides of any sort on your patch. Even organic pest controls kill, and just because something is natural, doesn't mean that it isn't toxic. Some of the most powerful poisons such as cyanide and ricin are found in plants and could be accurately labelled as natural or even organic! When it comes to pesticides, remember that anything that is designed to kill something has the potential to kill other things. So weedkillers applied to what some regard as pesky weeds will also kill other plants too.

In the same way, insecticides are formulated to kill insect pests, but these are not selective and will of course affect any insects that feed on the plants or come into contact with the actual spray. You've probably read or heard about neonicitinoids (neonics) these are powerful, systemic pesticides that are taken up by the plant and remain active within the plant against sap sucking pests. Of course pollinators don't suck sap, but they do collect pollen and nectar from flowering plants that could have been treated in this way. Bees accumulate pollen and nectar in their nests, so miniscule amounts of toxins can become concentrated and these poisons have sub lethal effects, meaning that they affect the bees without necessarily killing them. For bumblebees for example, research has shown that neonics can reduce the number of daughter queens that a colony produces, thus affecting future generations (Ref 89). Some garden centre plants labelled as pollinator friendly have been shown to contain cocktails of these chemicals, (Ref 90) making them unsuitable and potentially lethally toxic for pollinators, despite their labelling. Without detailed traceability of plants from cutting to mature plant it is impossible to know exactly what any plant has been treated with. The message is getting through and there have been bans and moratoriums on some of these toxins in agriculture and horticulture (for the very latest updates have a look online). The more people demand to know what their plants have been treated with before purchase, the quicker the message will sink in and the faster we will get pesticide-free ornamentals. To be safe buy organic plants from nurseries that can tell you what their plants have been treated with. Or grow from seed and take cuttings from plants that are mature and have not been sprayed with chemicals. In most garden scenarios there are always alternative ways to deal with perceived pests and problems without resorting to pesticides. For the sake of the bees, never use systemic insecticides of any sort in your garden.

CHAPTER SEVEN

Bee-good Plants

Bees and plants have evolved together over the millennia and many have complex and intricate relationships. There are specialist bees that only feed on specific types of plants, and there are generalist bees that use all manner of flowering plants to sustain their existence.

A quick check on the Internet will reveal lists and lists of plants that are good for bees, but these lists are massively overproduced and not always based on genuine observation or even science. If you aren't clued up about plants, then lists can be very confusing and not that helpful.

But there are some plants that are brilliant for all types of bees and when you are short on space, or you want to give the bees a real feast and not just a light snack, these are some of the best ones to grow.

FIND OUT MORE

There's been a lot of research recently on what plants are good for bees. Scientists from various organisations including Kew Gardens, The RHS and National Botanic Garden in Carmarthenshire, Wales have been studying which plants are good for pollinators.

BEE SAFE

RosyBee Plants (*Ref 91*) grows and sells organic plants that are great for bees, and also researches and studies which flowers and plants attract and support our pollinators. There is masses of information on the website and if you are in the UK you can order tried and tested bee-good plants direct from the nursery.

Remember that the best plants to grow for your local bees will vary from place to place. If you have a large area to plant then spend a bit of time visiting gardens near you at different times of the year and pay attention to those that are bee magnets (i.e. plants that attract lots of bees). Use your ears as well as your eyes and home in on the buzz. I'm convinced the sound is healing; perhaps it resonates on a specific frequency but whatever it is I am truly hooked.

You can pack a lot of bee-good plants into a border of perennials. © Martin Mulchinock

BEE AWARE

But remember that it's not as simple as going to the garden centre to buy plants for your bees. Unfortunately some plants available for sale have been pre-treated with systemic chemicals (including the dreaded neonicotinoids) to keep them free from pests and diseases and the really bad news is that the presence of these pesticides, even in very small doses can and does affect pollinator health. The best way to avoid this is to use an organic nursery that grows plants without the need for pesticides. It's easier to find organic edible plants that we might eat, e.g. fruit, herbs and vegetables, but the demand for organic ornamental plants is growing. There are some specialist organic plant nurseries out there, and even some that sell plants for bees (*Ref 92 and 93*); seek them out and support them as they are making a difference.

Grow from seed. This gives you a greater choice of plant varieties and more plants for your money, so it's ideal for sharing and increasing the bee-friendly plants in and around your area. You can even share or give away excess seed to make the very most of every seed in every packet.

Take cuttings from bee-good plants and share them far and wide. If you've got a great bee plant that can be propagated from, this is the ideal way to fill your garden with more bee plants and spread bee love by giving them as gifts to fellow gardeners. You don't have to tell them that it is a good plant for bees, just get them to plant it and the bees will come.

SPREAD THE WORD

Giving bee-friendly plants as impromptu gifts is a great way to spread pollen and nectar-rich plants. Even if the recipient isn't a bee fanatic, by planting your gift outside they are helping the bees. Encourage them to take cuttings or save seed and give more of this plant away to their friends to keep the process going. Imagine it as a positive form of pyramid selling without the greed, without exchanging money and with the benefit and health of the bees in mind. Make it into a fun project and see how far you can take it. It will be the bees and other pollinators that benefit the most, but spreading the love of gardening, plants and nature benefits everyone too. You can do it with seed too, saving seed from your favourite bee plants and popping them into thank you cards, birthday cards and any letters you might send. Keep a few for the Christmas crackers (and Christmas card list) and take them to meetings to share with friends or anyone you think might grow them. If there's a seed swap near you, spread the bee-love there and if you feel able and brave enough, give a talk and share your passion.

SIMPLY THE BEST

There's one group of plants that are particularly good for bees. If I mentioned echiums, the chances are you'd imagine the great spires of *Echium pininana* that you might see on your holidays in Cornwall or the Isle of Wight or in protected walled gardens around the UK. This echium is truly a stunner but it's not fully hardy and will not reliably overwinter in most UK gardens without some help. Each plant is tall and has thousands of individual flowers all up the flower spike that are really, really, really rich in nectar. The bees just love it, and it flowers for weeks and weeks. Look out for it at flower shows; there are one or two specialist growers. If you buy two-year-old plants they may flower the same year and create masses of bee food for your favourite insects. But the plants will die after flowering so it's essential to save seed and remember that the resulting seedlings will take two or more years to flower. Echium World (*Ref 94*), an expert in these plants, advises that *Echium pininana* can take three to four years to flower. They dig them up for the winter and take them in to a protected, cool glasshouse until the weather improves, protecting them with fleece in the coldest weather and unwrapping them on the sunnier days.

But there is a winter hardy, UK native echium that grows wild in some places and is commonly called viper's bugloss (*Echium vulgare*). It's related to borage and grows wild in most of Europe on coastal cliffs, waste ground and dry calcareous grassland and heaths (*Ref 94*).

It's a biennial which means that when you grow from seed the first year, the plant just grows leaves and gets a bit bigger, and it doesn't flower until the summer of the second season. But your plants will self-seed all over the place each year, taking two growing seasons to reach maturity and flower. They will pop up in the gravel paths, between the paving and all over the place. Great! Pot them up, grow them on and plant them all around the garden.

Viper's bugloss flowers for months and is a magnet for all pollinators that collect the soft blue pollen and sugar-rich nectar. You can grow it in pots where the spires of rich blue flowers will fountain over the edges and look beautiful.

EASY FROM SEED

There are many annual and biennial garden plants that are really easy to grow from seed and that are good for bees and pollinators, such as borage, nasturtiums and calendula.

You can sow and grow these by literally throwing the seeds over raked soil, or by planting in pots of compost outside in the garden. If sowing from seed really scares you then buy the plants from a nursery or garden centre. It's very likely that these plants will self-seed around your garden next year, providing random bee cafes in unexpected places. If the plants themselves can 'sow' and 'grow' their own plants from seed, you can do it too!

The UK native Echium vulgare is an excellent plant to grow in containers, borders and raised beds. © Jean Vernon

EASY FROM SEED

Borage is an amazing plant for bees. It's an annual herb worthy of any garden, and the pretty blue flowers are great for summer. The reason it's such a good bee plant and so popular with the little buzzers is because its flowers replenish their nectaries regularly, every two minutes (*Ref 95*) or so, so it's an open all hours nectar bar with generous supplies of the sugary nectar and this makes the flowers a magnet for bees all summer. Grow borage from seed, but once you've got it, it will self-seed around the garden. Look out for seed of white flowered borage, which is a pretty alternative.

Let the Phacelia flower around the edges of your veg patch, your flower garden and on any bare soil so that it will feed the bees. It's a good filler in the flower border too. © Jean Vernon

Phacelia (also called fiddleneck) is an amazing, blue flowered annual that is a fantastic plant for bees. It is usually grown as a green manure, which means that the plants are sown over bare soil after crops have been harvested and then cut back and dug into the soil to feed and condition the soil in spring. It's a great green manure because it grows fast and germinates in cold weather, but for best results it's dug back into the soil before it flowers. That's no good for the bees and other pollinators that simply love its flowers. If you want to grow it for the bees, then sow the seed into a generous patch of bare soil in a sunny spot any time from spring to autumn and let it grow and flower. Its soft mauve blue flowers are rich in pollen and nectar and if you

The clusters of tiny, nectar-rich flowers of Verbena bonariensis *are a magnet for pollinators who can land atop and drink from the sky nectar bar. © Martin Mulchinock*

THE SECRET LIVES OF GARDEN BEES

look closely at foraging bees, you will notice the blue pollen balls that they collect from these flowers.

Verbena bonariensis (purple top) is a great choice for gardens and for bees. It has airy see-through stems with purple flowers that mingle perfectly with other border perennials. A good strong clump of verbena will bear tufts of tiny flowers all clustered together in an easily accessible mass, creating a landing pad atop the tall wiry stems. This doesn't seem to put off huge bumblebees that cling to the swinging mass of flowers, supping from each individual bloom until almost drunk from the nectar. It's a great pollinator plant and is also a butterfly magnet and will attract a wide variety of these beautiful ethereal creatures.

Leave the seed heads on the plant at the end of the summer for this plant is yet another of the great self-seeders, spreading itself widely into gravel paths and nooks and crannies and of course into the garden soil. It is widely available from nurseries, garden centres and plant sales, so the easiest way to get these plants started in your garden, or in pots and containers, is to buy ready grown plants. But for the very best value for money these plants are really easy to grow from seed for lots and lots of plants, which you can divide up and plant *en masse* in your garden.

SPREAD THE LOVE

Don't forget that the more bee-friendly plants you can get into neighbouring gardens or gardens of people that aren't really interested in bees the further you are spreading your good work and providing food for bees and other pollinators in places where there might be little else.

Cosmos

If there's one summer flower that you can grow really easily from seed for the bees that will also be a great cut flower and border stalwart, the cosmos has to be top of the list. It's the perfect flower for bees because it has that flat open dinner plate kind of daisy-like flower, with pollen and nectar rich centres and plenty of room for several bees to feed at a time.

These are great garden plants with masses of flowers from June to October and very popular with butterflies and bees.

You can buy plants after the last frost in mid late spring, or buy a packet or two of seeds. Choose the easy to grow *Cosmos bipinatus*, in a mix of single open flowers, and sow the seeds in mid April onwards into pots of good quality seed compost, sprinkling the seed thinly over the surface and covering with a thin layer of compost. Germinate in a frost-free place and plant out after the last frost has passed.

The pretty cosmos plant has flowers for the garden, flowers for the house and flowers for the bees. © Martin Mulchinock

HERBS FOR BEES

Growing herbs is a fantastic way to start growing your own food. The simple practice of cutting a few leaves from herb plants in the garden and bringing them in to the kitchen to enhance a menu, jazz up a sandwich or transform a salad is a giant step for health, happiness and wellbeing. It's a great way to get everyone hooked on gardening. Herbs are not only pretty easy to grow but you might not realise that many herbs are brilliant bee plants too.

Marjoram

Wild marjoram, which seeds itself all around my garden, is ablaze with bees and other pollinators all summer, right into autumn. It's a pretty herb with rich emerald green or golden leaves and clusters of dusty pink, purple and sometimes white flowers. It's hailed as one of the best bee plants for good reason; the flowers are very rich in quality nectar providing an excellent sugary fuel for the bees for several months over summer. The short but abundant flowers make it a good general nectar source for bees of most types and explain why it is alive with butterflies, bees and hoverflies throughout the season. It's easy to grow, not fussy about the soil it grows in, but it likes a sunny spot. The plants grow to about a foot (30cm) tall and establish into clumps that regrow from a ground level crown each spring. The leaves are a tasty herb, ideal for pizzas, pastas and soups, and can also be dried for winter use.

You don't need a herb garden to grow marjoram, it will thrive in a pot in a sunny spot and offer valuable nectar to the garden bees. © Jean Vernon

Rosemary

This is one of my favourite herbs. First of all it is evergreen, keeping its leaves through the depths of winter. This means there are always rosemary leaves to add to your winter menus, make herbal tea and lift your spirits on the darkest days with its wonderful uplifting fragrance. Rosemary is a really good bee plant.

Gently remove a rosemary flower and sup the nectar from the end nearest the plant and you will get a sweet hit of rosemary nectar and understand its attraction to the bees. © *Jean Vernon*

The nectar rich flowers are a magnet for spring bees, searching for sustenance. In a sheltered spot rosemary plants can flower in late winter and early spring and sometimes in autumn and early winter too. This means it can provide vital bee food out of season.

It loves a hot dry spot with well-drained soil and unfortunately it can succumb to a hard winter, so it's always worth having a few cuttings growing in a sheltered spot to replace any losses.

Thyme

When it comes to bees, thyme is a very interesting plant. First it's a great source of nectar for our native bees and also for honeybees. It's also a very useful culinary plant, with leaves that are tasty and strong in flavour and used in a variety of savoury dishes. But thyme is also hailed as an extremely powerful medicinal plant. Renowned for its antimicrobial, antifungal and anti parasitic properties, thyme has a unique history as a heal-all plant.

Thyme oil based products are even used by some honeybee keepers as a treatment for the varroa mite.

It's a popular bee plant, which you will see as soon as it starts to flower. The tiny pink blooms are a magnet for bumblebees, butterflies and honeybees. Like the mint (and it's from the same family), the short tubular flowers are accessible by most species of bees and the quality of the nectar is good. It's another summer flowering plant, but is very low growing so it's ideal for pots and containers. Thyme is easy to grow and a great choice for a sunny spot on your patio or terrace.

Thyme is a low growing plant forming cushioning carpets of flowers that when mature are a mass of tiny, nectar rich flowers, heaven-sent for bees. © Martin Mulchinock

CHAPTER EIGHT

Season by Season in the Bee Garden

SPRING BEES

It might be getting warmer, but the danger for bees in early spring is the cold snaps that arrive after a warm spell. As the sun starts to warm the soil and the overwintering spots for bumblebees and solitary bees, these delicate creatures start to stir. They have been in a state of almost suspended animation for many months and will emerge on warm sunny days. Look out for any bee activity in your garden.

The large, fluffy, flying golf balls flying around the garden are the queen bumblebees. They have one thing on their mind, to make a nest and start a family. But first they have to find food and choose a safe place to site their nest.

To sustain all this activity the queen bumbles need to find nectar. You'll find them visiting all sorts of spring flowers in your garden, but favourites are the crocus and willow. The sugar rich crocus nectar will keep them going while they go about their business. But pollen is also essential, helping to ripen the eggs in their ovaries before they are laid inside a suitable nest.

Even little pots planted with crocus can make a difference to queen bees searching for food in spring. © Jean Vernon

House Hunting

Most bumblebees will nest in cavities underground. Look out for the large fluffy queen's tell tale zig-zagging flight path low to the ground as they search for just the right nesting spot.

Old mouse and vole holes are a favoured site and the bees have a remarkable way of finding them. Bees see in the UV spectrum and rodent urine fluoresces under UV light, so the bees can actually see where rodents have been.

These rodent nests are often already furnished with moss and bedding and as the tunnels and burrow have been prepared earlier it makes less work for our queen bees. She's got more than enough to do.

You'll see these queen bees with fat balls of pollen on their back legs, as they gather the protein-rich granules for their nest. Inside Chez Bumble the young mum-to-be will make a pea-size ball of pollen with an indentation in the top. At the entrance to the nest she will make a wax pot

If you see a large bee flying back and forth low to the ground and sometimes disappearing into holes, it's a queen bumblebee looking for the right place to make her nest. © Brigit Strawbridge Howard

from wax that she secretes from her body. It's shaped like the 'Winnie the Pooh' honey pot and will be filled with nectar that she collects from the nearby flowers. Close to the entrance it saves every morsel of energy as she empties her honey stomach after every foray until the pot is full. This is her emergency fund, literally for a rainy day. For once she has laid her first batch of eggs into the pollen ball indentation she will stay atop to keep them warm.

KEEPING WARM

Bumblebees have a remarkable way of heating themselves up and can do this even on cold mornings. They have very powerful flight muscles that operate their wings and keep them airborne, but these muscles can also be used to warm the thorax if they are disengaged from the wings and vibrated to raise their body temperature. This is how the queen bee incubates her first clutch of eggs.

Sweet Treat

The nectar pot, when filled, will sustain her through the incubation period and allow her eggs to hatch into little grubs. The pollen ball is the larval food that will sustain them until they weave their own silken cocoon and pupate inside into an adult worker bee.

There's no such thing as a baby bee; there are larvae and adults. The adult bees emerge fully formed and although the first brood bees are usually smaller than the later broods (the queen struggles to do everything and the first bees are often poorly fed), these worker bees, all female, are the first generation to take over housekeeping and foraging for the nest. It's a community, and once the first workers are ready and able to forage the queen bee can concentrate on laying eggs, which the workers then nurture and feed. Throughout spring, inside the bumblebee nest the queen lays worker eggs, the more the better, for they can forage far and wide and provision the queen and all the offspring with food.

Indie Bees

But it's not just the queen bumblebees that are alight in our gardens. The solitary bees are emerging too and they have even more to do than the bumblebees. Unlike the bumblebees that mate at the end of the season, before they go into winter torpor (insect hibernation), the solitary bees mate in spring. First to emerge from the nests are the males of the species. Not only does this mean that when the females emerge there are plenty of male bees to ensure that mating is successful, but it also gives the males time to check out the territory, mingle with other bees and disperse a little. This helps to ensure that the bees don't interbreed too much and helps increase the genetic biodiversity of the population. It also means that the males are at the very front of the nest and if the nest is attacked by a predator the females are safer at the back and less likely to be devoured. Ingenious evolution at its best. So you might see male solitary bees of some of the early emerging species such as the lovely Hairy-footed flower bee and some of the mining bees too.

Don't forget, if you have placed an insect house inside a sheltered shed for the winter, make sure you bring it back outside in early spring so that the emerging bees can start their new life cycle outside in your garden.

BEE RESCUE

Look out for ailing bees of all sorts in your spring garden (or at any time of the year). Foraging bees can quickly become exhausted. They might be trapped inside and have run out of energy at a window trying to get out. Or they could be at ground level having run out of fuel to complete their journey. Wherever they are you can help.

First quickly make a small solution of sugar syrup, one part water to one part sugar. Dissolve the sugar by stirring and gentle heat. Do not boil or allow to get too hot. Cool quickly by placing a small amount in a large metal spoon. Check the temperature. Once cool, take a tiny amount in a teaspoon. If the bee is in a safe place, put a drop or two of sugar solution in front of its face. It will quickly soak it up with its tongue. If she drinks the droplets, give her some more, but don't touch her, don't breathe on her and don't get the sugar solution on her.

If the bee is in a dangerous place then either stand guard while you administer your bee rescue, so she won't be stood on, or you will need to move her. Gently persuade her onto a dry spoon or a leaf or twig and move her to a safe place. Once she has taken some bee rescue solution she will quickly take off and resume her activities. If you save a queen bee or even a female solitary bee, you are potentially saving hundreds, if not thousands. For each one, if it successfully makes a nest and produces daughter queens/females, could secure the future generations of that species. Every bee counts.

A word of warning though – don't feed ailing bees honey. Although you might think that a drop of honey would be better than sugar (and actually some is), supermarket honey can contain the spores of some deadly bee diseases. You can't see the spores, but if you feed them to a wild bee it can and will take any disease spores present back to its nest. Better to err on the side of caution and give a fast food fix to get your bee flying again than risk giving it another problem to deal with.

Keep a little jar of sugar syrup in your day bag so that you can administer bee rescue when needed while out and about. © Shutterstock/VictoriaElizabethPalmer

Tree Blossom

As spring progresses the tree buds start to burst and spring blossom lights up our gardens. Established trees full of flower are an excellent source of pollen and nectar for spring bees building their nests. So much so that on warm sunny days when the nectar flow is strong, whole trees can come alive with the buzz of activity as bees of all species sup the available nectar. The busy as a bee mantra is in full effect and the close proximity of hundreds of flowers in one place makes an excellent fast food diner for these industrious creatures.

Spring blossom in the hedgerows is often the first to burst, but the early flowering cherries are quick to follow, with apple, pear and almond flowers bursting in quick succession. Sharp cold snaps can knock the flowers back, resulting not only in a drop in food for our bees, but also poor pollination of our trees and subsequently low fruit yields in our gardens. By planting a succession of spring flowering trees (and shrubs), not forgetting those with rich pollen supplies, you will make a huge difference to your local bee populations that will grow year on year.

Currants for Bees

If you have borders in your garden where you can plant a few shrubs, this is a great way to introduce low maintenance, permanent structure to your borders and provide bee cafes specialising in pollen and nectar. One established shrub covered in flowers offers a great filling station for our pollinating friends and it's a great place to stake out to watch the bee activity in your garden. On my plot there are a few shrubs that flower early offering a rich source of nectar.

One of the best is the flowering currant (*Ribes sanguineum*) in shades of pink to red that are a magnet for bumblebee queens in the spring. A medium sized bush will be covered in clusters of flowers, each cluster of flowers arranged like a bunch of grapes hanging from the stems. Stake it out and see what bees visit; it's the perfect place to do a bee count or just practice identifying queen bumbles. The short tubular flowers are accessible for most bees, though some of the longer tongued bees may avoid it. In my garden it is particularly popular with queens of the Early bumblebee (*Bombus pratorum*).

EARLY SPRING PERENNIALS FOR BEES

Late winter and early spring are the most critical times for our bees, whether it's the overwintering honeybees first venturing out on a sunny day or the emerging queens and solitary bees; once the weather starts to warm the garden comes alive with pollinators searching for food. The trouble is that the weather can be very unpredictable and a warm spell that lures the queens from their torpor can just as quickly turn to cold. Unless there are sufficient nectar and pollen rich flowers for these early risers to forage on they are in deep trouble. Even plants that are naturally up and flowering in winter can stop providing nectar and pollen in a cold snap, especially when covered in snow or hard frost. Establish a handful of great early spring perennials that are also bee-good plants to sustain your winter bees. Once your clumps are mature you can experiment by forcing part of a plant with cloches for earlier flowers, leaving the rest to its natural flowering time, or pot up cuttings and bring them on in the greenhouse so that when they flower you can place them outside for the bees. These perennials will bridge the gap from winter into spring and provide for the garden bees for several weeks or months until spring starts in earnest.

Hellebores

Hellebores are almost designed for bees with their nodding flowers and virtually bottomless nectaries to attract our fluffy friends. The large bell shaped flowers create shelters for the feeding bees in poor weather and there's a wide range of species that flower from Christmas (*Helleborus niger*) right into spring, offering your wild bees a generous menu of energy rich nectar to get them going. These elegant flowers are a vital resource and each one keeps its nectaries provisioned for up to three weeks, making these plants excellent for emerging queen bumblebees and other wild bees as well as the honeybees. What's more, the flowers contain plenty of protein-rich pollen, essential for feeding the developing brood of wild bees and honeybees early in the season.

Pulmonaria (Lungwort)

Lungwort is a great late winter, early spring plant for bees. The leaves are spotted and slightly hairy but it's the nectar-rich flowers that attract the bees, appearing in February and March as the queen bumbles emerge and start to provision their nests.

Pulmonaria is a slow spreader forming low cushions of leaves and flowers in spreading clumps. Let it grow and if you are lucky you will attract one of the prettiest solitary bees that seems to have a preference for its flowers. The Hairy-footed flower bee is as described. The male is a fluffy, gingery yellow haired bee, the female black, and both with feathery legs, and they simply love lungwort. It's a good way to spot them as they hover around pulmonarias in flower, darting about like hummingbirds and barely stopping long enough to feed. It's a woodland plant so it tolerates some shade.

Perennial Borage (*Trachystemon orientalis*)

Don't be put off by the botanical name of this plant. It is also known as perennial, oriental borage and that's a very fair description of this plant. It has clusters of soft mauve and white flowers that look very much like borage flowers with the petals turned back. Any early emerging bees are attracted to its blooms and you can often hear the plants buzzing with activity in the depths of winter.

If you've got dry shade and a bit of space, plant this amazing perennial borage, it's a spring bee bar and the flowers are loaded with nectar. © Martin Mulchinock

It's closely related to borage and it's a fantastic winter flowering source of nectar for bees. To be honest it rarely features on bee plant lists and that's a real puzzle because it's a good garden doer if you have the space.

It flowers when there is so little else in flower in the garden and depending on the weather it can start to flower anytime from December through to March. Plus it's a perennial so once you've planted it; it will come up year after year. The only downside is that it does spread, which if you have a small garden it might not be the best choice for your plot, but you could grow it in a large planter. Keep it under control by dividing it regularly and sharing the divisions with other bee-loving gardeners.

SUMMER BEES

As summer follows spring, the bee season is well underway and your garden will be alive with the sound and sight of bees busily foraging on your plants and provisioning their nests with pollen and nectar. The bumblebees that have successfully nested in spring will have raised their first brood and these worker bees take over, leaving the queen bee to lay more eggs that the new workers will now raise. The bee activity in your garden will start to increase, there will be more mouths to feed and the worker bees will be foraging hard.

Inside the bumblebee nests the worker bees will hatch and build up and by midsummer the nests will be peaking with many foraging bees bringing pollen and nectar back to the nest. These bees will fly from dawn to dusk, providing that it is not very windy, very wet or very hot.

In adverse weather conditions the bees will rely on their emergency nectar pots stored inside the nest to sustain them until the weather improves.

In very hot weather you may notice fewer bees in your garden. That's because they get too hot in the sun, especially bigger bumblebees, and struggle to regulate their temperature. Instead they may remain in their cooler nest and feed on the emergency stores, choosing to forage in the early morning and later at night when it is cooler.

If you have a bumblebee nest you may see bees outside the entrance fanning their wings; they do this to improve the air flow in the nest and to evaporate water to cool the nest.

Remember that in hot dry weather plants will produce less nectar if there is no rain, and the bees will struggle to feed themselves. Water key bee plants that you know are being visited to keep the nectar flowing.

Nesting

In the flower border you may see all sorts of solitary bees foraging for pollen. The Leaf-cutter bees will be harvesting leaf sections to seal their nests, the Wool carder bees will be shaving hairs off the stachys plants to line their nests and many of the other species will be provisioning their nests with pollen and searching for mud or other materials to seal their egg chambers.

Keep an eye for nesting activity in and around your insect house. © *Martin Mulchinock/Marc Carlton.*

THE SECRET LIVES OF GARDEN BEES

Keep a muddy puddle wet in the summer months for the bees and other wildlife to gather nest-building materials. Mason bees and some birds use mud to help build or seal their nests.

Look out for solitary bee nests; it's a great time to watch these fascinating creatures tooing and froing from nesting sites. They will be gathering pollen to provision their eggs so you may find them on pollen-rich flowers, and nesting in insect houses.

Boy Bands

As summer progresses the bumblebee nests will produce a generation of male bumblebees, who will be evicted from the nest as soon as they hatch. You will find these bees hanging about in the flower garden, supping on nectar and waiting for the girls.

Look out for them overnighting in flowers, or languishing on nectar-rich flowers where they can feed while waiting for their bride, as the workers from their nest continue to forage.

When the daughter queen bees hatch in the summer bumblebee nest, the boys are ready for action. You may be lucky to witness bumblebees mating in your garden in mid to late summer. After the mating season, the male bees will gradually die off and the original nest and original mother queen bee will eventually die too. This year's mated daughter queens will be in your garden feeding themselves up on nectar, so you will see beautiful freshly emerged queen bees on your bee-good plants. You may also see them at ground level searching for a place to overwinter. Occasionally these daughter queens will forgo overwintering and establish a new nest straightaway, and this will give rise to late season foraging bees and winter active colonies. This is more likely in the southern counties of the UK.

HOW TO HELP THE BEES IN SUMMER

Look out for solitary bee nests in your lawn and stop mowing those areas while the mother bee makes her nests. You might see small mounds or volcanoes of sifted soil scattered around small pencil thin holes. The bees will take a few weeks to finish provisioning their nests. Give them space, keep the dog away and observe from a distance. See if you can identify the species and if it's something rare then do record it with BWARS.

Go on a bumblebee safari with a bee savvy expert and learn more about these bees. It will help you identify a few of the more common bees in your garden and you can find out a bit more about these amazing creatures. The Bumblebee Conservation Trust (*Ref 96*) runs a number of events each year. They are very popular so keep a watch on the website for events or follow them on Twitter or Facebook.

Go low mow and leave a patch of your lawn to flower. The additional area of wildflowers will provide a rich variety of forage for bees of all types.

Stake out bee holes in your lawn or garden and see what is nesting there. Take pictures to identify later. © *Jean Vernon*

Plant more summer flowers. If you've got the room then plant up a bee border with some bee delights planted *en masse* for your buzzy friends. Choose plants that will grow and flower year on year like lavender and catmint and other summer perennials. If you plant three great bee plants for each season and add to them each year you will continually improve the forage for your local bee population.

- Do the Chelsea Chop – when you've got an established clump of a flowering perennial, such as catmint, campanula, phlox, penstemon or similar, consider cutting a third of it back around the time of Chelsea Flower Show, in mid to late May. This is a technique called the Chelsea Chop and basically delays flowering for some of your plant. This staggers the forage available for your bees, providing some later flowers in June when there is sometimes a dearth of bee plants in flower (see June Gap below).
- Water your plants – in order to make nectar, plants need to be well watered. That's easy if there's been plenty of rain, but a longer spell of hot dry weather will not only dry out the ground, it will also affect the nectar supplies.
- Put out a bee drinker – bees need water too. They will sip it in the shallows of a garden pond, or precariously balance on the edge of a bowl of water, gathering precious drops of water to cool the colony by evaporation. A birdbath of marbles or sea beans filled with rainwater provides safe drinking places and adds an interesting feature to the garden.
- Sow seeds of biennial bee magnets like foxgloves, viper's bugloss and honesty in July and until late summer so that they will flower next season for your bees.

The June Gap

It's a well-known phenomenon that between the early blush of spring and the flora of mid summer there's often a long gap in flower production in our gardens, meadows and greater landscape. The trees have mostly finished flowering, the spring bulbs and perennials have finished and the summer flowers are yet to bloom. It's known as the June Gap and coincides with the building up of bumblebee colonies and the nesting activities of solitary bees.

Deadhead Your Plants

Remove any fading and spent blooms regularly to keep your plants flowering. Many will keep on making new flowers in an effort to form seed and will flower for longer. Some of the best plants to grow to span the June Gap are roses. Although roses rarely provide nectar they are rich in pollen. You need to choose wild roses, like the dog rose and some of the species roses, or single varieties where the centre of the flower is accessible to the bees. Highly bred double roses have the stamens tightly covered in layers of petals making the pollen virtually unavailable to the bees.

AUTUMN

Late summer into autumn is a wonderful time in the garden. When it comes to bees there are still plenty out and about in our gardens foraging for pollen and nectar. And there are lots of fabulous plants still in flower.

Some of the solitary bees have two generations of offspring in one year, which means there may be new nests and foraging adults within your garden. But there is one solitary bee that appears as autumn starts: the Ivy bee. It nests in sandy soils and when it starts to emerge in September the first bees to appear are the males who fly fast and frantically over the nest entrances of other Ivy bees close to their own nest. Sometimes they are in such numbers that you might think it's a large nest, or even a swarm. Solitary bees don't swarm and what you are seeing is the frantic search by the males for a female. Like most solitary bees the males hatch first, disperse a bit and then await the emergence of their females.

Their food plant, the common ivy (*Hedera helix*), is in flower. It's a vital source of nectar for many autumn active bees and for the Ivy bee it is it's main source of food. Let it flower if you possibly can. Leave it clambering over old walls and sheds where its stems provide essential nesting sites for birds. Even the black berries are a useful source of winter food for some bird species.

The super stripy Ivy bee puts in an appearance in early autumn, emerging from underground nests, sometimes in large numbers. © Liam Olds

Hidey Holes

The daughter queen bees from this year's bumblebee nests will be mated by autumn and will be feeding up before their winter torpor. These female bees need to find a safe place to overwinter and will burrow into friable soil, compost heaps and north facing banks where they will spend several months in a sort of suspended animation. A north-facing bank doesn't get the warmth of the sun until spring arrives and wakes these sleeping beauties from their slumber.

Inside the solitary bee nests the eggs will have hatched into larvae, which will feed on the store of pollen provided by the mother bee and then weave a cocoon around themselves where they will pupate during their transformation from larvae to adult bee.

HOW TO HELP THE BEES IN AUTUMN

Many bees will still be foraging and feeding up, so ensure you have some late summer, autumn flowers such as the very bee-friendly ice plant (*Sedum spectabile* now called *Hylotelephium spectabile*), autumn flowering asters and the wonderful coneflowers (*Echinacea*) that start flowering in summer and keep going into late autumn too.

- Keep removing dead flowers from any flowering plants to encourage a few last blooms into autumn.
- Leave a patch of lawn to flower for the late feeding carder bees.

The cone flowers smell of honey and attract bumblebees to feed from their central boss. © Martin Mulchinock

- Buy some organic spring-flowering bulbs and plant them in pots and containers or into your flower borders. These will root over the winter and start to grow in early spring offering your garden bees a vital source of early pollen and nectar.
- Don't be too hasty to cut down plants in the border that have finished flowering. Seed heads provide food for wild birds and dead/hollow stems can create overwintering or nesting places for some bees. Even the faded foliage can protect the plant crowns from extreme cold through the winter.
- Autumn is a great time to assess your garden plants and see what you can add to the garden to help the bees. If you've got a large plot then consider planting some trees and shrubs that will mature to provide the bees with a significant source of pollen or nectar.

WINTER BEES

If you think that winter is a tough season for us, think about the wildlife in your garden. Feeding the birds is one way to help support creatures through the winter, but spare a thought for the garden bees. While you may not see very many through the winter months, that doesn't mean they are not present, eking out their survival from the resources collected from your garden through spring, summer and autumn.

Honeybees are perhaps the species you are most likely to see over the winter, on mild, still days when the temperature reaches 7–8°C. Even though they should have vast reserves of their winter food (honey) stored within their hive, they will still foray outside when the conditions are right.

Bumblebee queens can start emerging in the midst of winter if there is a warm spell of a few days or more. If the weather continues to be mild and plants start to emerge

and flower, these bees will gather essential food and start to make a nest. The most common bumblebees seen in mid to late winter are the Early bumblebees (*Bombus pratorum*), the Buff-tailed bumblebee (*Bombus terrestris*) and the White-tailed bumblebee (*Bombus lucorum*). These are the early emergers and will be searching for nest sites and food.

The problems start when a warm spell is followed by another cold snap

Queen bumblebees overwinter in small cavities in the ground. © BBCT

and wintery conditions prevail. Unless these bees have made a nectar store already, many will perish. Look out for ailing queen bees that have become still and immobile and are apparently in trouble. You can give them an energy boost and a helping hand with a sugar solution (see bee rescue).

If you live in the southern counties of England and Wales you may see worker bumblebees and male bumblebees in January and February. This is unusual activity and should be recorded. The bees are usually the Buff-tailed bumblebees and are a sure sign that a queen bee has foregone hibernation after mating in late summer, and instead started a new nest at the end of the season. The workers foraging and the emergence of the males is a sign that this nest has been successful and that a second generation has overwintered nearby. This is undoubtedly a result of climate change and in a mild winter may give the newly emerged daughter queens the chance to set up a spring/summer nest.

HOW TO HELP THE BEES IN WINTER

- Go careful in the winter garden, especially when brandishing your trowel or fork, for nestling in cavities within the soil, moss and woodpiles are a variety of overwintering queen bumblebees. Each one has filled its belly with food to sustain it through the cold, bleak midwinter, waiting for the temperatures to rise and spring to arrive. Many will shelter in north-facing banks and borders where the winter sun fails to warm the soil, thus preventing them from emerging too early, but even still a few days of fake spring can bring many out of their torpor state and into life in your garden. Watch out for their early activity and be ready with your trusty bee rescue remedy to administer to ailing queens.
- If you unearth a sheltering queen, be sure to put her carefully back to where you found her, or if that's not possible find a small terracotta flowerpot and fill the bottom with dried leaves. Place the bee inside and fill to the top with more leaves, placing the pot on its side in a sheltered, north-facing position in your garden.
- All queen bumblebees and emerging solitary bees also need to quickly find a rich source of pollen to mature their eggs before they can start laying their first brood. This protein-rich material is essential to ensure that their ovaries and eggs within can ripen. They also need nectar to sustain them through these early, frantic weeks as they look for a suitable nest site and prepare to nest.
- Plant winter flowering shrubs and early flowering perennials and bulbs to provide a source of food.
- Force some early spring flowers into life to ensure that there are nectar and pollen sources in your garden. Bring pots of spring flowering bulbs into the greenhouse or an outbuilding and gently water them. When they are about to flower place them outside for early pollinators to find.

- Don't start moving firewood and log piles around and keep away from bee shelters and piles of garden debris. All will undoubtedly be home to a variety of pupating solitary bees that have been provisioned by last year's females and are now in a state of almost suspended animation, waiting for spring to arrive when they will emerge. Keep these impromptu bee houses and shelters protected from rain and snow, as it is not the cold that is the enemy of these little creatures, but the damp and the rain if it seeps into their winter abodes.
- Keep a check on firewood to avoid burning overwintering solitary bees. Wood that has started to rot or has woodworm holes is the perfect nesting material for many of the small, solitary bee species. Leave it outside.
- Clumps of snowdrops or crocuses can be brought into flower a week or two earlier by placing a cloche over them as they push their way through the soil. Don't force them all, just ensure there are a few healthy clumps open for when the bees start to emerge looking for food.
- Plan and plant for next winter, choosing plants that are in flower now and that are attracting bees and pollinators locally. Visit local open gardens and listen for the fabulous sounds of bees collecting nectar and pollen. These are the plants that are vital for the bees in the midst of winter. Many are scented and add that extra fragrant dimension to the winter garden.
- Clear a space for a wildflower patch in the garden and order some wildflower seeds or a meadow or flower lawn mix.
- Order your seeds for the year, choosing plants with single flowers where the pollen and nectar are accessible, and open-pollinated plants (not F1 hybrids) so you can save the seed and grow them again and share with others.
- Have a seed swap with like-minded friends and share seeds of bee-good plants. Plan a plant swap for spring where you can swap surplus plants or sell to raise funds for a bee charity.
- If growing from seed scares you or you don't have the time or space to do so, then order some organic bee-friendly plants from a specialist nursery. Get together with other bee-loving friends and do a bulk order so that you can share the plants and the delivery costs.

Further Reading

My reading pile to learn about bees just grows and grows, not only with the limitless supply of scientific research, bee-centric websites and entomologist blogs but also with a range of fabulous books.

The following books are an essential read to learn more about identifying bees and bee behaviour. There are plenty more that you will find when you dip into the subject, but these are a good place to start.

Dancing with Bees: A journey into Nature, Brigit Strawbridge Howard, Chelsea Green Publishing 2019.

Field Guide to the Bees of Great Britain and Ireland, Steven Falk, Richard Lewington, British Wildlife Publishing Ltd, 2015, Bloomsbury Wildlife Guides.

Solitary Bees, Ted Benton, Pelagic Publishing, Naturalists' Handbook 33.

New Naturalist Bumblebees, Ted Benton, HarperCollins, 2009

RSPB Spotlight Bumblebees, Richard Comont, Bloomsbury.

Bumblebees: An introduction, Nikki Gammans, Dr Richard Comont, S C Morgan, Gill Perkins *Bumblebee* Conservation Trust

A Sting in the Tale, Dave Goulson, Vintage Jonathan Cape Ltd, 2014

The Humble-Bee: Its Life-history and How to Domesticate it, with Descriptions of All the British Species of Bombus and Psithyrus, Frederick Sladen.

Citizen Science/Get Involved

Get involved in bee walks, bee counts and projects that need gardeners to observe, record and share their bee experiences to further the knowledge base for garden bees. The Bumblebee Conservation Trust relies on volunteers to gather data on the distribution and the abundance of bumblebees via its BeeWalk (*Ref 97*) Scheme. It also runs a variety of bee safaris and identification courses to train volunteers and other interested people and offers support and advice.

Taking part in a bee survey or safari can get you up close to a range of amazing bees.
© Jean Vernon

THE SECRET LIVES OF GARDEN BEES

For beginners the iSpot website (*Ref 98*) is a good place to start as it offers identification advice via a free community. You upload your images and others help with the identity. It can be plants, trees, bees or any other wildlife and it's a good place to hone your ID skills.

The value of this data is when it is collated, as once you've got your bee or other insect identified you can add it to iRecord (*Ref 99*) which then confirms the information and shares it with the National Biodiversity Network (*Ref 100*) that shares and exchanges the information with its members.

Download a bee identification app on your smart phone, such as the 'Blooms for Bees' app. You can get involved in surveys to discover which flowers are good for bees and to help understand the foraging activity of bumblebees in gardens and allotments. 'Blooms for Bees' (*Ref 101*) also has a recording system for bees on line and some bee identification guides.

Friends of the Earth is the largest grassroots environmental campaigning community in the UK. One of its campaigns is 'The Bee Cause' (*Ref 102*), designed to help save bees. It helped bring about the restriction of the use of bee-harming neonic pesticides on outdoor crops in the UK and the EU and helped persuade the Welsh and UK governments to draw up national Bee Action Plans, the first in the world. It also coordinates The Great British Bee Count to collect data on bee species around the UK.

Natural Beekeeping Trust (*Ref 103*) offers an alternative approach to the care of honeybees that works with the natural behaviour of the honeybee and focuses on the colony of the bees, rather than the production of honey.

The Buzz Club (*Ref 104*) encourages its members to conduct fun and educational projects and become pollinator researchers. It's all about the bees and other pollinators and a great place to start for youngsters.

The UK Bees, Wasps and Ants Recording Society (BWARS) (*Ref 105*) is a subscription-based volunteer recording society which aims to promote the recording of the aculeate (stinging insects) of the Hymenoptera in Great Britain and Ireland.

BugLife (*Ref 106*) is actively working to save Britain's rarest little animals (the invertebrates) from bees to beetles, worms to woodlice and jumping spiders to jellyfish. It raises awareness, develops protective legislation, encourages conservation and undertakes practical conservation projects such as creating B-Lines (*Ref 107*) or insect pathways to join up existing wildlife areas.

PlantLife (*Ref 108*) works nationally and internationally to raise the profile of the open spaces of our nature reserves, to celebrate their beauty and to protect their future. With bees and plants inextricably linked the work of PlantLife and the preservation of wildflowers and wildflower habitat is an essential cog in the huge wheel of protecting and saving the wild bees.

The Centre for Ecology & Hydrology (CEH) operates a Pollinator Monitoring and Research Partnership (*Ref 109*) with surveys to establish how insect pollinator populations are changing across Great Britain. Volunteers can get involved in counting pollinators. A survey pack is available online.

References

1. Canadian Honey Council
2. RHS Advice
3. https://www.bumblebeeconservation.org/
4. http://www.bumblebee.org/hort.htm
5. http://www.bumblebee.org/hort.htm
6. http://www.bwars.com/bee/apidae/bombus-lapidarius
7. http://www.bwars.com/bee/apidae/bombus-lapidarius
8. http://www.bwars.com/index.php?q=bee/apidae/bombus-pascuorum
9. https://www.bumblebeeconservation.org/ginger-yellow-bumblebees/great-yellow-bumblebee/
10. http://www.bwars.com/index.php?q=bee/apidae/bombus-distinguendus
11. *Bombus monticola*, BWARS Species Page, Edwards, M, 2012. www.bwars.com.
12. *Bumblebees: behaviour, ecology and conservation*, Goulson, D, 3rd Ed., Oxford University Press, 2010
13. https://www.foe.co.uk/sites/default/files/downloads/bees_north_east.pdf
14. https://www.bumblebeeconservation.org/short-haired-bumblebee-reintroduction-project/
15. *A Sting in the Tale*, Dave Goulson, Vintage Jonathan Cape Ltd, 2014
16. https://www.bumblebeeconservation.org/short-haired-bumblebee-reintroduction-project/
17. Distribution and floral preferences of the rare bumblebees *Bombus humilis* and *B. soroeensis* (Hymenoptera: Apidae) on Salisbury Plain. Goulson, D. & Darvill, B., *British Journal of Entomology and Natural History*, 16:95–102,   2003
18. http://www.wbrc.org.uk/WORCRECD/issue_29/Bombus_humilis_Worcs.html
19. Goulson & Darvill 2003
20. https://www.bumblebeeconservation.org/red-tailed-bumblebees/shrill-carder-bee/
21. https://www.buglife.org.uk/bugs-and-habitats/shrill-carder-bee
22. Studies on Scandinavian bumble bees (Hymenoptera, Apidae), Løken, *Norsk entomologisk Tidsskrift*, 1973
23. *Hummeln: bestimmen, ansiedeln, verwahren, schützen.* E. von Hagen, Naturbuch Verlag, Weltbild Verlag GmbH, Augsburg, 1994

24. https://www.bumblebeeconservation.org/bee-faqs/bumblebee-nests-frequently-asked-questions/
25. Visual and Olfactory Floral Cues of Campanula (*Campanulaceae*) and Their Significance for Host Recognition by an Oligolectic Bee Pollinator), Milet-Pinheiro P, Ayasse M, Dötterl S. https://www.ncbi.nlm.nih.gov/pubmed/26060994
26. http://www.wildlifetrusts.org/reserves-wildlife/guide-solitary-bees-britain
27. http://www.bwars.com/index.php?q=bee/andrenidae/andrena-nitidiuscula
28. *Field Guide to the Bees of Great Britain and Ireland*, Steven Falk, Richard Lewington, British Wildlife Publishing Ltd, Bloomsbury Wildlife Guides, 2015
29. Falk, & Lewington, 2015
30. http://www.wildlifetrusts.org/reserves-wildlife/guide-solitary-bees-britain
31. http://www.bwars.com/bee/apidae/eucera-longicornis?page=1
32. John Walters Notebook; http://johnwalters.co.uk/notebook/post.php?s=2014-06-30-longhorned-bees
33. http://www.bwars.com/content/submit-sighting-colletes-hederae-ivy-bee
34. BWARS information sheet, Warncke, 1973
35. Comparative Study on the Biology of Macropis fulvipes(Fabricius, 1804) and Macropis europaea, Warncke, *Folia biologica (Kraków)*, vol.52 (2004), No 1-2A, 1973
36. Waldemar Celary http://www.isez.pan.krakow.pl/journals/folia/pdf/52(1-2)/13.pdf
37. BWARS information sheet by Stuart Roberts: http://www.bwars.com/sites/www.bwars.com/files/info_sheets/10_anthidium_manicatum_1col_infosheet.pdf
38. BWARS information sheet by Stuart Roberts
39. http://www.bbc.co.uk/programmes/p02tcrqt
40. Falk, & Lewington, 2015
41. https://www.flickr.com/photos/63075200@N07/sets/72157633013852384/
42. BWARS info sheet, http://www.bwars.com/sites/www.bwars.com/files/info_sheets/chelostoma-campanularum-info-sheet.pdf
43. https://www.flickr.com/photos/63075200@N07/sets/72157633013852384/
44. http://www.edphillipswildlife.com/the-harebell-carpenter-bee-chelostoma
45. https://www.ncbi.nlm.nih.gov/pmc/articles/PMC4465695/
46. NHM – Insect Information Service
47. Steven Falk Flickr Megachile
48. BWARS Information Sheet/ http://www.bwars.com/sites/www.bwars.com/files/info_sheets/05_Anthophora_plumipes_1col_infosheet.pdf
49. BWARS Information Sheet/ http://www.bwars.com/sites/www.bwars.com/files/info_sheets/05_Anthophora_plumipes_1col_infosheet.pdf
50. https://www.youtube.com/watch?v=kmskSVfnw8A

51. https://www.bumblebeeconservation.org/hairy-footed-flower-bee-anthophora-plumipes/

52. www.naturalbeekeepingtrust.org

53. Quote – keeping honeybees to save the bees is like keeping chickens to save the birds – unknown origin

54. *Smelly Male Bumblebees*, Cathy Horsley, Conservation Officer BBCT, https://www.bumblebeeconservation.org/smelly-male-bumblebees/

55. Goulson, 2014

56. Bumblebees can discriminate between scent-marks deposited by conspecifics, Richard F. Pearce, Luca Giuggioli & Sean A. Rands. https://www.nature.com/articles/srep43872

57. RSPB Spotlight bumblebees – Richard Comont

58. https://www.darwinproject.ac.uk/commentary/life-sciences/tale-two-bee

59. http://www.bwars.com/bee/megachilidae/chelostoma-florisomne

60. https://www.livescience.com/1643-bees-favorite-color.html

61. http://www.abc.net.au/news/science/2016-11-16/birds-and-bees-prefer-have-flower-colours-preferences/7959382

62. https://en.wikipedia.org/wiki/Bombus_polaris

63. http://www.bwars.com/index.php?q=content/winter-active-bombus-terrestris-data-gathering

64. https://www.sciencedaily.com/releases/2015/09/150901204819.htm

65. Synergistic effects of floral phytochemicals against a bumble bee parasite, Palmer-Young et al, *Ecology and Evolution*, 2017, https://onlinelibrary.wiley.com/doi/full/10.1002/ece3.2794

66. Parasitized bees are self-medicating in the wild, Dartmouth College, *ScienceDaily*, 1 September 2015. www.sciencedaily.com/releases/2015/09/150901204819.htm

67. https://www.sciencedaily.com/releases/2015/09/150901204819.htm

68. Detection and Learning of Floral Electric Fields by Bumblebees, Clarke, Whitney, Sutton & Robert. *Science* http:/dx.doi.org/10.1126/science.1230883

69. Dynamic Nectar Replenishment In Flowers Of Penstemon (Scrophulariaceae), Maria Clara Castellanos, Paul Wilson, James D. Thomson https://www.csun.edu/~hcbio028/pubs/CAS_000C.PDF

70. Hidden poisons in rhododendron nectar https://www.kew.org/blogs/kew-science/hidden-poisons-rhododendron-nectar

71. https://www.bumblebeeconservation.org/bee-faqs/finding-dead-bees

72. Charles Darwin, cats, mice, bumble bees and clover, Carreck, Norman; Beasley, Toby; Keynes, Randall. (2009). *Bee Craft.* 91. 4–6.

73. https://www.darwinproject.ac.uk/letter/DCP-LETT-607.xml

74. https://www.darwinproject.ac.uk/commentary/life-sciences/tale-two-bees

75. Falk & Lewington, 2015

76. The aliens in the 1979 film *Alien* by Ridley Scott were inspired by the lifecycle of parasitoid insects.

77. http://nurturing-nature.co.uk/award-winning-solitary-bee-nesting-box/

78. Stephanie O'Connor, https://dspace.stir.ac.uk/bitstream/1893/20348/1/2014%20 Steph%20Thesis%20ii.pdf

79. *Bumblebees*, Free, J.B. and Butler, R.F., Collins Press; London, 1959

80. *The Humble-bee*, Sladen, F.W.L., Macmillan and Co. Ltd., Hereford, UK, 1912

81. *Bumblebees*, Benton, T., HarperCollins Publishers, London. 2006

82. https://dspace.stir.ac.uk/bitstream/1893/20348/1/2014%20Steph%20Thesis%20ii. pdf

83. Falk & Lewington, 2015

84. An Introduction to Trigger Plants, Rica Erickson, Australian plants online.

85. Festival of Nature, Tom Timberlake, Bristol University

86. https://www.nature.com/articles/srep34499?WT.feed_name=subjects_evolution

87. https://en.wikipedia.org/wiki/Acanthus_mollis

88. Do linden trees kill bees? Reviewing the causes of bee deaths on silver linden (Tilia tomentosa), Hauke Koch and Philip C.Stevenson, RBG Kew, https:// royalsocietypublishing.org/doi/full/10.1098/rsbl.2017.0484

89. In 2017 CEH (Centre for Ecology & Hydrology) published the results of a large scale field realistic experiment to assess neonicitinoid impacts on honeybees and wildbees across Europe, in the peer-review journal *Science*. Woodcock et al, 2017

90. http://sro.sussex.ac.uk/67224/ Ornamental plants on sale to the public are a significant source of pesticide residues with implications for the health of pollinating insects

91. http://www.rosybee.com

92. Bee Happy Plants is a great resource in the UK. www.beehappyplants.co.uk

93. There's a useful list of other nurseries and suppliers on the RHS Website https:// www.rhs.org.uk/advice/profile?pid=960

94. http://www.echiumworld.co.uk/

95. Goulson, 2014

96. Bumblebee Conservation Trust- www.bumblebeeconservation.org

97. http://www.beewalk.org.uk/

98. https://www.ispotnature.org/communities/uk-and-ireland

99. https://www.brc.ac.uk/irecord/

100. https://nbn.org.uk/

101. http://www.bloomsforbees.co.uk/

102. https://friendsoftheearth.uk/bees

103. https://www.naturalbeekeepingtrust.org/

104. http://thebuzzclub.uk/

105. http://www.bwars.com/content/about-bwars-introduction
106. https://www.buglife.org.uk/about-us
107. https://www.buglife.org.uk/b-lines-hub
108. https://www.plantlife.org.uk/uk
109. https://www.ceh.ac.uk/our-science/projects/pollinator-monitoring

Index